and Questioning Students and Families

The needs and rights of lesbian, gay, bisexual, transgender, and questioning (LGBTQ) students and families are often ignored, generally misunderstood, and only rarely given priority by the school system. This book provides a practical and useful guide for school-based mental health professionals to support students, families, teachers, and administrators in the development of a safe, inclusive school environment for all LGBTQ students and families. It begins with an overview of the unique issues and challenges faced by LGBTQ students and families, including a discussion of sexuality and gender identity development within the interconnected contexts of home, school, and community. Practical steps are given for creating an inclusive school environment; implementing prevention and intervention techniques to address discrimination, bullying, and violence; and organizing effective counseling programs for LGBTQ students. These school-based efforts are then extended to working with families and communities to reinforce steps taken in the school context. An accompanying CD includes numerous handouts, sample letters, and other resources to assist the school-based mental health professional in implementing responsive and affirmative practices for LGBTQ students and families.

Emily S. Fisher, PhD, is an Associate Professor in the School Psychology Program at Loyola Marymount University.

Kelly S. Kennedy, PhD, is an Assistant Professor in the School Psychology and School Counseling Programs at Chapman University.

Routledge
Taylor & Francis Group

School Based Practice in Action Series
Series Editors
Rosemary B. Mennuti, EdD, NCSP
and
Ray W. Christner, PsyD, NCSP
Philadelphia College of Osteopathic Medicine

This series provides school-based practitioners with concise practical guidebooks that are designed to facilitate the implementation of evidence-based programs into school settings, putting the best practices *in action*.

Published Titles

Assessment and Intervention for Executive Function Difficulties
George McCloskey, Lisa A. Perkins, and Bob Van Divner

Resilient Playgrounds
Beth Doll

Comprehensive Planning for Safe Learning Environments: A School Counselor's Guide to Integrating Physical and Psychological Safety - Prevention through Recovery
Melissa A. Reeves, Linda M. Kanan, Amy E. Plog

Behavioral Interventions in Schools: A Response-to-Intervention Guidebook
David M. Hulac, Joy Terrell, Odell Vining, and Joshua Bernstein

The Power of Family-School Partnering (FSP): A Practical Guide for School Mental Health Professionals and Educators
Cathy Lines, Gloria Miller, and Amanda Arthur-Stanley

Implementing Response-to-Intervention in Elementary and Secondary Schools: Procedures to Assure Scientific-Based Practices, Second Edition
Matthew K. Burns and Kimberly Gibbons

A Guide to Psychiatric Services in Schools: Understanding Roles, Treatment, and Collaboration
Shawna S. Brent

Comprehensive Children's Mental Health Services in Schools and Communities
Robyn S. Hess, Rick Jay Short, and Cynthia Hazel

Responsive School Practices to Support Lesbian, Gay, Bisexual, Transgender, and Questioning Students and Families
Emily S. Fisher and Kelly S. Kennedy

Forthcoming Titles

Serving the Gifted: Evidence-Based Clinical and Psycho-Educational Practice
Steven I. Pfeiffer

Ecobehavioral Consultation in Schools: Theory and Practice for School Psychologists, Special Educators, and School Counselors
Steven W. Lee

Everyday Program Evaluation for Schools: Implementation and Outcomes
Diane Smallwood and Susan G. Forman

Pediatric School Psychology: Conceptualization, Applications, and Leadership Development
Thomas J. Power and Kathy L. Bradley-Klug

Early Childhood Education: A Practical Guide to Evidence-Based, Multi-Tiered Service Delivery
Gina Coffee, Corey E. Ray-Subramanian, G. Thomas Schanding, Jr., and Kelly A. Feeney-Kettler

Responsive School Practices to Support Lesbian, Gay, Bisexual, Transgender, and Questioning Students and Families

Emily S. Fisher ■ Kelly S. Kennedy

Routledge
Taylor & Francis Group

NEW YORK AND HOVE

First published 2012
by Routledge
711 Third Avenue, New York, NY 10017

Simultaneously published in the UK
by Routledge
27 Church Road, Hove, East Sussex BN3 2FA, UK

Routledge is an imprint of the Taylor & Francis Group, an informa business

Library of Congress Cataloging in Publication Data
Fisher, Emily S.
    Responsive school practices to support lesbian, gay, bisexual,
    transgender, and questioning students and families / Emily S.
    Fisher & Kelly S. Kennedy.
    p. cm.
    Includes bibliographical references and index.
    1. Sexual minorities. 2. Sexual minority students. 3. Social work
    with sexual minority youth. 4. Sexual minority parents.
    I. Kennedy, Kelly S. II. Title.
    HQ73.F57 2012
    306.874086'6—dc23
    2012001659

ISBN: 978-0-415-89073-1 (hbk)
ISBN: 978-0-415-89074-8 (pbk)
ISBN: 978-0-203-82915-8 (ebk)

Typeset in Melior
by EvS Communication Networx, Inc.

SUSTAINABLE
FORESTRY
INITIATIVE

Certified Sourcing
www.sfiprogram.org
SFI-00555
The SFI label applies to the text stock.

Printed and bound in the United States of America by
Walsworth Publishing Company, Marceline, MO.

Contents

Series Editors' Foreword

The *School-Based Practice in Action* series grew out of the coming together of our passion and commitment to the field of education and the needs of children and schools in today's world. We entered the process of developing and editing this series at two different points in our career, though both in phases of transition. One (RWC) moving from the opening act to the main scene, and the other (RBM) from main scene to the final act. Despite one of us entering the peak of action and the other leaving it, we both continue to be faced with the same challenges in and visions for education and serving children and families.

Significant transformations to the educational system, through legislation such as the No Child Left Behind Act and the reauthorization of the Individuals with Disabilities Education Act (IDEA 2004), have had broad sweeping changes for the practitioners in the educational setting, and these changes will likely continue. It is imperative that as school-based practitioners we maintain a strong knowledge base and adjust our service delivery. To accomplish this, there is a need to understand theory and research, but it is critical that we have resources to move our empirical knowledge into the process of practice. Thus, it is our goal that the books included in the *School-Based Practice in Action* series, truly offer resources for readers to put directly "into action."

To accomplish this, each book in the series will offer information in a practice-friendly manner and will have a companion CD with reproducible and usable materials. Within the text, readers will find a specific icon that will cue them to documents available on the accompanying CD. These resources are designed to have a direct impact on transitioning research and knowledge into the day-to-day functions of school-based practitioners. We recognize that the implementation of programs and the changing of roles come with challenges and barriers, and as such, these may take on various forms depending on the context of the situation and the voice of the practitioner. To that end, the books of the *School-Based Practice in Action* series may be used in their entirety and present form for a number of practitioners; however, for others, these books will help them find new ways to move toward effective action and new possibilities. No matter which style fits your practice, we hope that these books will influence your work and professional growth.

Working with Emily Fisher and Kelly Kennedy on this important and timely project of supporting LGBTQ students and families in our schools has been a delight. In this book, *Responsive School Practices to Support Lesbian, Gay, Bisexual, Transgender, and Questioning Students and Families*, Fisher and Kennedy provide us with a strong knowledge base about LGBTQ students and families, as well as offer practical strategies for school-based practice. It is comprehensive and addresses various school personnel, including mental health providers, teachers, administrators, and parents. Through the use of four case examples integrated throughout book the authors offer useful and helpful information and guidance to help us support LGBTQ students and families. Although this is not a simple issue to address within school settings, Fisher and Kennedy furnish school-based professionals with the needed knowledge and tools for schools to be open and responsive in a sensitive and effective manner. We are delighted to have this resource be a part of the *School-Based Practice in Action* series, and we trust this will be a valuable resource for those working in schools.

Finally, we want to extend our gratitude to Mr. Dana Bliss and Routledge Publishing for their support and vision to develop a book series focused on enriching practice and service delivery within school settings. Their openness to meet the needs of school-based practitioners made the series possible. We hope that you enjoy reading and implementing the materials in this book and the rest of the series as much as we have enjoyed working with the authors on developing these resources.

Rosemary B. Mennuti,
EdD, NCSP

Ray W. Christner,
PsyD, NCSP

One

Lesbian, Gay, Bisexual, Transgender, and Questioning Students and Families

The unique needs and school experiences of lesbian, gay, bisexual, transgender, and questioning (LGBTQ) students have been long recognized by researchers. However, it is only within the last few years that the plight of this minority group has received more widespread public attention, with media coverage of devastating events (i.e., suicide and homicide) raising the alarm for many educators and advocacy groups. Along with these tragedies, there has been an overall increase in the visibility and acceptance of LGBTQ individuals in the media and increased attention to divisive political battles over equal rights issues (e.g., gay marriage). In fact, it can be difficult to keep up with the continual shifts between acceptance and controversy that characterize society's stance toward the LGBTQ community, but this much is clear: LGBTQ issues are gaining a powerful momentum, and educators need to get on board in recognizing and responding to the needs of LGBTQ students and families.

Terminology

There is no one right way to refer to LGBTQ individuals (although there are plenty of wrong ways), and the primary idea is to use respectful and inclusive language. Throughout this book, lesbian, gay, and bisexual (LGB) refer to an individual's sexual orientation (physical and emotional attractions), transgender (T) refers to an individual's gender identity (or

1

sense of self as a boy or girl), and questioning (Q) refers to an individual who is not yet sure how he or she identifies. As a whole, this group can be referred to as a sexual (LGB) and gender (T) minority. Iterations of these terms/acronyms are used throughout the literature, sometimes with other variations included (e.g., "I" is sometimes added to include intersex). More information on sexual orientation and gender identity can be found in Chapter 2. In this book, the acronym LGBTQ will be used except when research is clearly focused on certain sub-groups (e.g., LG or LGB).

LGBTQ Students

LGBTQ students experience alarmingly high rates of harassment, bullying, and discrimination at school based on their sexual orientation or gender identity (Birkett, Espelage, & Koenig, 2009; Crothers, 2007; Kosciw, Greytak, Diaz, & Bartkiewicz, 2010). Added to the normal tumultuousness of adolescence, these experiences can lead to a number of problematic outcomes, such as higher rates of depression, substance abuse, and suicide (Espelage, Aragon, Birkett, & Koenig, 2008; Kosciw et al., 2010). Similarly, the impact of a hostile school climate where LGBTQ students feel unsupported and unprotected can lead to poorer school outcomes, such as skipping school, earning lower grades, and reporting fewer educational aspirations (Birkett et al., 2009; Kosciw et al., 2010). More information about school factors in the lives of LGBTQ students can be found in Chapter 3, along with information about home and community influences. The CD contains a facts sheet on LGBTQ students in schools and other contexts (with materials for Chapter 3).

LGBTQ Parents and Their Children

Parental involvement is seen as critical to students' success, and parents who identify as LGBTQ are highly involved in their children's schooling (Kosciw & Diaz, 2008). However, some parents can feel marginalized by the school system, hearing anti-LGBTQ language at school, failing to have their family structure recognized during classroom activities, and not feeling welcomed by teachers and other school staff (Kosciw & Diaz, 2008). Similarly, children from LGBTQ-parented families often hear negative comments about LGBTQ individuals from other students and school staff, get teased because of their parents' or their own sexual orientation or gender identity (actual as well as perceived), and fail to have their families fully recognized as valid and valuable (Kosciw & Diaz, 2008). The experiences of LGBTQ parents and their children can be found in Chapter 9, along with information about how schools can be more welcoming and responsive to them. A fact sheet on LGBTQ parents and their children is on the accompanying CD (with materials for Chapter 9).

Developing Responsive School Practices

The bad news is that schools often fail to be inclusive and supportive places for LGBTQ students and families. Fortunately, there is a lot that school personnel can do to change this. Taking steps to create a supportive climate that fosters academic, social, and emotional development for LGBTQ students and families requires knowledge and a commitment to action. Accurate information about sexuality and gender identity development (addressed in Chapter 2) and the various factors that impact LGBTQ youth in home, school, and community contexts (Chapter 3) provide the groundwork for understanding and responding to this diverse group. School personnel can be more responsive and inclusive of LGBTQ students and parents by putting foundational policies in place (addressed in Chapter 4), improving school climate by responding to and preventing bullying and harassment (addressed in Chapter 7), providing professional development for teachers (addressed in Chapter 5), promoting sensitivity and appreciation for diversity among students (addressed in Chapter 5), improving classroom climate (addressed in Chapter 6), integrating LGBTQ issues into classroom curriculum (addressed in Chapter 6), providing mental health support services (addressed in Chapter 8), supporting families (addressed in Chapters 9 and 10), and connecting with community resources (addressed in Chapter 11). Change is not easy, but sometimes all it takes is one person who can envision a world where this book is obsolete.

Case Studies

Throughout this book, four case studies will be used to illustrate principles and practices. The complete case studies, with information from the appropriate chapters, are on the accompanying CD.

Sarah

Sarah is an eighth-grade student attending a large, racially and ethnically diverse, progressive middle school in New York City. Sarah has always earned good grades and is very active in extracurricular activities. Sarah is well liked by her peers and teachers. Sarah is biracial—her father is Caucasian and her mother is African American. About six months ago, Sarah started telling people that she is bisexual. This has not seemed to affect her peer relations, as Sarah was recently elected vice-president of her class. Sarah's parents, who consider themselves liberal, have met with Sarah's school counselor, Mr. Martin, to discuss Sarah's disclosure of her sexuality. They confided in him that they think this might just be a phase Sarah is going through, and they are confused by Sarah's revelation of being bisexual, because, as far as they know, she has not had any sexual contact with boys or girls. They are concerned that she is not considering the long-term ramifications of telling people she is bisexual because it is really a private matter and she might change her mind in the future.

More on Sarah can be found in Chapters 2, 6, 10, and 11.

Javier

Javier is a twelfth grade student attending a large high school in Dallas, Texas. Javier is a first generation Mexican American, as are most students in his school. Javier is an average student who plans on attending community college when he graduates. Javier's mother recently discovered text messages with sexual content between Javier and another boy (who does not attend Javier's high school). When she confronted Javier, he told her that he thinks he is gay. Javier's mother broke down crying and begged Javier not to tell anyone else about this. She told him that he would tear the family apart if he acted on these feelings. The following day, she talked to the school social worker, Mrs. Santos, to tell her what happened and to ask her to talk to Javier about not being gay.

More on Javier can be found in Chapters 8, 10, and 11.

Sydney

Sydney is a second grade student new to her school this year. Her school is in a small town located in the outskirts of Oklahoma City, Oklahoma. On the first day of school, Sydney's father, Mr. Green, brought the school psychologist paperwork from the previous school indicating an assessment plan had been signed at the end of the year to test Sydney for speech and language issues. The school psychologist asked Mr. Green to come in for a meeting to get more information about Sydney. At the start of the meeting, the school psychologist asked about Sydney's background, and her father was forthcoming about Sydney being adopted from China, that language delays were present since Kindergarten, and that her other developmental milestones had been met on time. The school psychologist noticed that Mr. Green became more reserved when he began asking about Sydney's home life. After several of his questions were met with minimal responses, he began asking more about Sydney's academic development and peer relationships. At the end of the meeting, they made plans to proceed with the assessment. Two weeks later, the school psychologist was called to the school office. Sydney had a headache and asked to call her father to come pick her up. The man who arrived was not recognized by the school staff and was not listed on Sydney's emergency card, but he was insisting he was Sydney's father. The school psychologist took Sydney into his office to ask her about the man who came to school. Sydney got very upset and confessed that she had "called the wrong dad" by mistake. When asked more about this, it became clear that Sydney lived with two dads at home, but was only supposed to talk about one of them at school.

More on Sydney can be found in Chapters 4, 6, and 9.

Jessie

Jessie is finishing eighth grade in a few weeks and will be starting ninth grade in a couple of months at a high school in Fresno, California. Jessie's parents have requested a meeting with the high school principal to discuss their expectations for how Jessie will be treated in high school. Jessie was born a boy but, since early childhood, he has identified as a girl. Over the last two years, Jessie, with the support of her parents, has begun living her life as a girl. This transition was met with a great deal of resistance in middle school. In addition to Jessie being harassed and bullied by her peers, one of Jessie's teachers told her that she was bringing the bullying on herself and she should just "act like a boy" if she wanted it to stop. Jessie's parents tried to work with the middle school administration, but they felt that their concerns were not adequately addressed and Jessie was not safe at school. They pulled Jessie out of school to homeschool her for the last half of eighth grade. Having heard about all the problems from the middle school principal, including pending litigation against the school, the high school principal requests that the school psychologist be present for the meeting and Jessie's parents agree to this. At the meeting, Jessie's parents want the school to develop a plan for how they are going to ensure that Jessie is integrated into the school community, that she is treated with respect and dignity by school staff and peers, and that she feels safe to "just be herself" at school.

More on Jessie can be found in Chapters 4, 5, 6, and 8.

Two

Development of Sexuality and Gender Identity

The concepts of sex and gender are complexly intertwined. Some define sex as a biological construct that categorizes an individual as male or female (e.g., chromosomes and genitalia) and gender as a social construct related to the expression of masculine or feminine characteristics (e.g., hair style and type of clothing). However, as more becomes known about sex and gender, such as variations in the typical male/female sex dichotomy, the distinctions between the two become murky. Instead of thinking of sex and gender as distinct constructs, one might see them as interrelated, continually affecting and interacting with one another as an individual develops from the time of conception through old age.

Brief Overview of Sexual Development

From birth, humans are sexual beings (DeLamater & Friedrich, 2002; Pluhar, 2009). During infancy and early childhood (approximately birth to 6 years), children display a natural curiosity about their bodies and the bodies of others. This often takes the form of touching or rubbing of the genitals, wanting to see other people's bodies, mimicking adult behaviors such as kissing or holding hands, and asking questions about bodies and bodily functions (DeLamater & Friedrich, 2002; Hornor, 2004; "Sexual Development and Behavior in Children," 2009). Children of this age generally have an openness with their bodies and feel comfortable being naked around others ("Sexual Development and Behavior in Children," 2009).

School-aged children (approximately 6–12 years) generally become increasingly modest with their bodies and want more privacy ("Sexual Development and Behavior in Children," 2009). They are more likely to engage in purposeful masturbation (usually in private), to include sexual content in their conversations and games with peers (e.g., Truth or Dare), and to be interested in pictures, television shows, and movies that show naked or partially naked people ("Sexual Development and Behavior in Children," 2009). Because children at this age socialize most frequently with same-sex peers, sexual exploration and learning at this age generally takes place within these groups (DeLamater & Friedrich, 2002). It is during this time that children generally experience their first sexual attraction and first sexual fantasies (Savin-Williams, 2005).

Puberty brings a host of physical changes, such as increases in sex hormones, genital maturation, and sexual interest (DeLamater & Friedrich, 2002), accompanied by psychological and emotional changes (Wolfe & Mash, 2006). There is quite a wide range of ages in which puberty begins, with girls typically starting earlier than boys (from 8–13 years old for girls; 9.5–14.5 years old for boys) (Noland, 2006). Timing of onset of puberty may impact boys and girls somewhat differently. For example, in boys and girls, early onset of puberty has been associated with increased risk behaviors (e.g., smoking, alcohol use, earlier sexual activity) (Wolfe & Mash, 2006). However, early maturing girls also experience greater psychological problems (e.g., depression, eating disorders) (Wolfe & Mash, 2006). Additionally, late onset of puberty for boys has been associated with school problems, increased depression, greater familial conflict, and increased risk for bullying (Wolfe & Mash, 2006).

Sexual Orientation and Sexual Identity Development

Increasing emotional and sexual intimacy is a natural part of adolescence (Wolfe & Mash, 2006). Generally, it is during adolescence that sexual identity and orientation emerge (DeLamater & Friedrich, 2002). Sexual identity and sexual orientation are separate but related concepts. Sexual identity is how an individual defines him or herself, while sexual orientation is defined by an individual's sexual attraction (both physical and emotional) (Auslander, Rosenthal, & Blythe, 2006). Although sexual identity in adolescence can be considered fluid due to the normal exploration that occurs during this time of life (Auslander et al., 2006), the stability of adolescent sexual identity should not be discounted as most individuals maintain their sexual identity through adolescence and early adulthood (Rosario, Scrimshaw, Hunter, & Braun, 2006). In most cases, sexual identity and sexual orientation align, although some adolescents may define themselves in a way that differs from their sexual orientation. For example, a teenage girl who is attracted to other girls (sexual orientation) may identify as straight (sexual identity) because she envisions herself marrying a man in the future.

For many heterosexual youth, the development of a sexual identity happens without much thought or consideration (Wolfe & Mash, 2006), and scholars have largely left the concept of heterosexual identity development unexplored. Conversely, much has been written about sexual identity development for lesbian, gay, and bisexual individuals, with several different models being proposed that typically involve progression through stages. Sophie (1985–1986) examined models of sexual identity development and outlined four key stages that encapsulated many of the models:

1. First awareness—characterized by feelings of differentness with some awareness of same-sex attractions, although these feelings are generally kept secret from others.
2. Test and exploration—characterized by individuals' mixed feelings about their same-sex attractions, initial but limited contact with LGB individuals, and feelings of isolation from the heterosexual community.
3. Identity acceptance—characterized by initial positive feelings about their sexual identity, a preference for socializing with other LGB individuals, and first disclosure of sexual identity to non-LGB individuals.
4. Identity integration—characterized by individuals recognizing the stability of their sexual identity, experiencing pride in their identity as LGB persons, being more open with others about their sexual identity, and feeling anger at societal prejudice.

As indicated in the first awareness stage above, in retrospective studies, most LGB adults have reported feelings of "differentness" as children that they later understood to be early indications of their sexual identity (Savin-Williams, 1996). It is most often during puberty that these feelings of differentness take on a sexual component, likely because this is when all adolescents are experiencing more intense sexual desires.

It is the self-recognition of same-sex attraction that often begins the coming out process, which has been described as "a process of small realizations, filled with forward and backward steps" (Savin-Williams, 1990, p. 34) rather than a one-time insight or event.

Savin-Williams (1996) described the coming out process as involving two distinct, yet related components: self-labeling and disclosure. Self-labeling is an internal process by which individuals become aware of attraction to same-sex individuals and begin to identify as lesbian, gay, or bisexual (even if only to themselves). Internally, individuals are trying to understand and integrate the view of themselves as LGB with previously held senses of self. Generally, after becoming more comfortable with self-labels, individuals may begin to disclose their sexual identity to others, the second aspect of coming out. First disclosure most often occurs with a best friend, with families being told at some later point.

A good resource to share with educators about sexual orientation and identity development is, "Just the Facts about Sexual Orientation and Youth: A Primer for Principals, Educators, and School Personnel" (Just the Facts Coalition, 2008), which is available on the accompanying CD.

Gender Identity Development

Gender identity is one's internal sense of his or her own maleness or femaleness, and it is generally thought that children develop their gender identity (the sense of themselves as boys or girls) by the age of 3 years (DeLamater & Friedrich, 2002; Hornor, 2004). This multidimensional construct involves biological, cognitive, and social influences (Galambos, Berenbaum, & McHale, 2009), and the development of an integrated gender identity (i.e., a stable sense of manhood or womanhood) is an important task of adolescence (DeLamater & Friedrich, 2002).

It is typical for young children to explore both gender roles through play; however, there are two groups of children who will likely encounter particular difficulty with gender identity development—those who are intersex and those who are transgender (Noland, 2006). Although these conditions occur quite infrequently, they can have a great impact on children and families.

Intersex

Intersex is a term used to describe a wide range of biological and genetic conditions that affect internal and external genitalia and/or sex hormones, making individuals fall outside of the typical male/female biological dichotomy (Denny & Pittman, 2009). The term *intersex* has replaced the term *hermaphrodite* in contemporary literature, as it captures a wider range of individuals with varying conditions (Rosario, 2006). Some intersex individuals are born with ambiguous genitalia, making it difficult to determine at birth if the individual is a boy or girl, while in others, the condition does not become apparent until later in life (e.g., during puberty when there is a surge in hormones) (Denny & Pittman, 2009). It is estimated that at least 1 in 1,000 individuals could be described as intersex (Vilain, 2006).

Lev (2006) described the typical process that occurs when babies are born with ambiguous genitalia (i.e., observable intersex condition). The children are assigned a sex at birth (i.e., boy or girl) by medical professionals, and the general medical protocol is for children to have surgery to align the appearance of their genitals with the assigned sex as soon as possible. Early sex assignment and subsequent surgery is done to reduce psychosocial trauma for the family and child. As children develop, they may need to take hormones to support their development in their assigned sex. Lev (2006) noted that there is some controversy surrounding genital surgery for intersex children, focusing on both ethical issues (e.g., informed consent) and efficacy issues (e.g., potential for misassignment or surgical complications).

Research suggests that intersex individuals experience a culture of silence around their condition, often feeling different but not understanding why (MacKenzie, Huntington, & Gilmour, 2009). These individuals report that key adults in their lives (e.g., parents, doctors) were not forthcoming in helping them understand their experiences (MacKenzie et al., 2009). Similarly, while intersex individuals generally identify with their assigned sex, some experience significant gender dysphoria (defined below) and uncertainty about their gender identity (MacKenzie et al., 2009).

Gender Dysphoria and Transgender

There is a small portion of the population whose gender identity (their internal sense of themselves as boys or girls) does
not match their biological sex. This is called *gender dysphoria*
and it can be mild (with some feelings of discomfort surrounding gender identity), or it can be more severe (with strong and
persistent feelings of discomfort with one's gender) (Zucker,
2006). For intersex individuals with gender dysphoria, incor-
rect gender assignment after birth may explain this discomfort. Non-intersex individuals with severe gender dysphoria
are often diagnosed with Gender Identity Disorder (GID). GID
is characterized by (Zucker, 2006; Zucker & Cohen-Kettenis,
2008):

- Extreme cross-gender identifications;
- Strong discomfort with one's biological sex or the gender
  roles of that sex;
- In adolescents, a belief that they were born the wrong
  gender and a desire to take actions to change their sex
  characteristics to match their gender identity.

Zucker (2006) noted that these feelings are not transient;
rather, these feelings are intense and persistent for the individual. These individuals may self-identify or be identified by
others as transgender, a broad term used to describe individuals (usually adolescents or adults) whose gender identity does
not match their biological sex. It is important to note that there
is controversy surrounding the idea that transgender individuals have a disorder (i.e., GID), as some believe that transgender is a normal variation of gender identity (in the way that it
is accepted by major medical and psychological organizations
that homosexuality is a natural variation of sexual identity)
(Zucker, 2006).

The prevalence of GID is difficult to estimate, but various
sources (e.g., adult clinical populations, indices on rating
scales) indicate that it is quite rare (Zucker & Cohen-Kettenis,
2008). Boys receive the diagnosis more frequently than girls,
likely due, in part, to greater social intolerance of cross-gender
behaviors in boys than girls (Zucker & Cohen-Kettenis, 2008).
Similar to the age range in which children develop their gender identity, parents of children and adolescents experiencing GID often report cross-gender behaviors during preschool
years (Zucker, 2006). However, as previously noted, many

young children explore both male and female gender roles during play, and this should not be considered pathological (Noland, 2006). It is when parents do not see their children "growing out" of these behaviors that they most often seek clinical help (Zucker & Cohen-Kettenis, 2008).

The developmental trajectories for those diagnosed with GID in childhood versus adolescence are different. For those diagnosed in childhood, GID is less likely to persist into adolescence and adulthood, while for those diagnosed in adolescence, GID is likely to persist into adulthood (Zucker & Cohen-Kettenis, 2008). As their gender identity becomes more integrated, adolescents and adults often begin to identify as transgender. It is important to note that those who experience gender dysphoria in childhood that does not persist into adulthood are substantially more likely to report an LGB identity in adolescence and adulthood (Zucker & Cohen-Kettenis, 2008).

The School's Role

Given that sexuality and gender identity are normal parts of development, they cannot be ignored in the school setting. It is not uncommon for Kindergarten and first grade teachers to have boys and girls who engage in some form of masturbation in the classroom. Third and fourth grade children will likely be excited (and also grossed out) by a first kiss in a story. Ask any middle school teacher, and you will get an earful about how raging hormones affect students during puberty. During high school years, dating, relationships, and sex take center stage in many adolescents' lives. School also provides the context in which all students, but especially those who identify as LGBTQ, understand their development in relationship to their peers. The remaining chapters of this book provide information and strategies for helping school personnel foster appreciation and acceptance of diversity and promote healthy development for all students.

Case Study

Sarah

After hearing the parents' concerns, Mr. Martin explains that it is typical for adolescents to explore different aspects of their identity, such as ethnic and sexual identity, as they move from childhood to adulthood. He tells them that it is possible that

Sarah will continue to develop and redefine her sexual identity throughout adolescence and early adulthood, but it is also possible that Sarah will maintain her bisexual identity. Mr. Martin ends the meeting by complimenting Sarah's parents by saying, "Listen, it's a testament to the safety and openness in your relationship that Sarah feels like she can talk to you about her sexuality. Could we meet again next week to talk more about how you might best communicate with Sarah about your questions and concerns?" Sarah's parents readily agree to talk more with Mr. Martin, and they also ask him if he will check in with Sarah's teachers to make sure there aren't any school problems developing.

Three

LGBTQ Students in Home, School, and Community Contexts

Like all students, LGBTQ students exist in multiple contexts that impact their development and outcomes. When discussing the various risk and protective factors in the lives of LGBTQ students, it is necessary to be clear that *being* LGBT or Q is not a risk in and of itself. Examining youth within their developmental contexts allows educators to discover that, when problems occur, they are most likely due to the fit of students with their environments (Orban, 2003), thus implying that the solution lies primarily within the environment, not within students. Youth have many environments that influence their development on a daily basis, from the obvious school, home, and community contexts to the less apparent societal and socio-political contexts. Adding complexity to this already multifaceted situation is the fact that many contextual factors can serve to either support or hinder students' development.

Risks

Due to a number of environmental factors, coupled with complex identity development issues (discussed in Chapter 2), LGBTQ students are at a greater risk than their heterosexual peers for a number of risky behaviors and problematic outcomes. The most common and pervasive risk faced by this group of students is victimization. Sexual minority students experience high rates of discrimination, verbal harassment, threats, bullying, physical assault, and social exclusion (Kosciw, Greytak, & Diaz, 2009). It is important to remember that these harmful behaviors are faced by both students who are "out" as well as those who are perceived by others as being outside of the heterosexual norm, despite students' true identity (Kozik-Rosabal, 2000). Research has directly linked discrimination and victimization to the various negative outcomes and risks known for this population (e.g., Marshal et al., 2008; Savin-Williams, 1994).

Risks faced by LGBTQ youth include both internalizing and externalizing behaviors and problems. Internalizing problems include low self-esteem, isolation, hopelessness, depression, and suicidal ideation/attempts (Cooper-Nicols & Bowleg, 2010; Hansen, 2007; Marshal et al., 2008). Rates of these behaviors can be considerably higher for LGBTQ youth than for heterosexual youth. For example, Safren and Heimberg (1999) found that approximately 30% of sexual minority youth attempted suicide, compared to 13% of their peers. Externalizing behaviors that LGBTQ youth are at elevated risk for include substance abuse, sexual risk behaviors, running away, truancy, aggressive behaviors, and police encounters (McGuire, Anderson, Toomey, & Russell, 2010; Resnick et al., 1997; Savin-Williams, 1994). These behaviors contribute to increased risk of academic failure, homelessness, and death (Savin-Williams, 1994).

Many researchers and scholarly works (including the present) collapse sexual minority youth into one term for simplicity. However, it is important not to forget the various groups and subgroups within LGBTQ, as some youth face higher risks than others. Studies have shown that bisexual (Kennedy & Fisher, 2010; Murdock & Bolch, 2005), transgender (Kosciw et al., 2009; McGuire et al., 2010), and questioning (Espelage, Aragon, Birkett, & Koenig, 2008) students may face higher rates of exclusion, victimization, isolation, and therefore higher rates of the negative outcomes associated with these factors. For example, lesbian and gay students are approximately 190% more likely to use drugs or alcohol than heterosexual youth, and bisexual youth are approximately 340% more likely (Marshal et al., 2008). Risks may also be different for youth based on their disclosure status (Hansen, 2007; Savin-Williams, 1994). In some cases, disclosure may bring needed attention and potentially protective resources (e.g., supportive adults, intervention in cases of harassment), and in other cases, disclosure may increase negative factors (e.g., harassment, rejection). Youth who have not disclosed their identities may experience guilt, shame, or internalized homophobia, and may be unable to access counseling or other supports to help with these feelings. On the other hand, youth who have disclosed may have access to these supports, but may face discrimination, harassment, or isolation if they are in unsupportive environments. Finally, sexual minority youth of color may face even higher rates of harassment and therefore more overall risks than other sexual minority and heterosexual peers (Potoczniak, Crosbie-Burnett, & Saltzburg, 2009).

Resilience

Overall, the elevated risks faced by LGBTQ students demand the attention of school personnel. However, educators are cautioned not to presume that risk rates or statistics can inform them of the exact circumstances of any given student or that every sexual minority student is troubled (Savin-Williams, 2005). Even with alarming rates of critical behaviors, such as suicidal ideation, it must be recognized that the majority of LGBTQ youth do not experience negative outcomes. Information regarding the pervasiveness of harassment and discrimination highlights the fact that LGBTQ youth who do not manifest unhealthy or risky behaviors have not developed in an absence of these factors, but rather in spite of them, demonstrating the importance of promoting resiliency (Holmes & Cahill, 2004; Mayberry, 2006). Additionally, when adults focus only on the negative outcomes or behaviors associated with this group, it may inadvertently perpetuate a negative stereotype that LGBTQ youth are "problem" students (Mayberry, 2006). Therefore, acknowledging the strengths of these youth is especially important.

In each of the contexts described in this chapter, students may encounter factors that increase risk or promote resilience (i.e., protective factors). Figure 3.1 provides a visual representation of many of the identified protective factors for LGBTQ students across the various contexts described in this chapter. Currently, research has identified significantly more risk factors than protective factors, often because risks were the only type of factors examined in studies. However, as new research begins to examine factors associated with both risky behaviors and resiliency, it is likely that more protective factors for LGBTQ students will be identified across contexts (e.g., Garmezy, 1993; Rutter, 2001). Additionally, when risk and protective factors have been researched for other topics, such as delinquency or mental health, scholars have created models to explain the interactions between risk and protective factors in terms of how they work to impact developmental

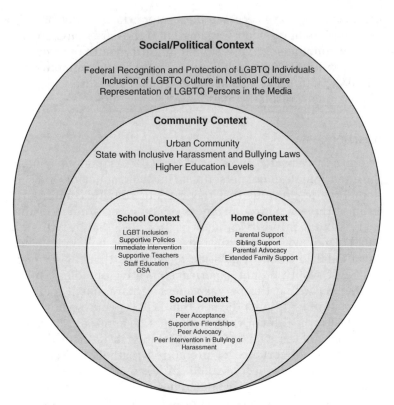

Figure 3.1   Protective factors for LGBTQ students across contexts.

trajectories. Currently, few studies regarding LGBTQ students have attempted to apply this approach (e.g., Szalacha, 2003), which may ultimately help school professionals to answer questions such as:

- What is the impact of a Gay-Straight Alliance (GSA) (a protective factor) on school-based risk factors?
- Which risk factors, when present, place students at the highest risk for suicidal ideation?
- Does a supportive peer context protect students from risks faced by having an unsupportive home context?

These questions illuminate the complexity involved when we try to examine contexts in terms of risk and protective factors. Currently, there are not conclusive answers to these questions, and, until more is known, it is best to take an individualized approach to understanding various elements impacting the lives of LGBTQ students. Through this approach, we can work with students and their families to minimize the presence of risks and increase the salience of protective factors across all contexts, with the goal of helping students to be resilient.

Home Context

Not all LGBTQ youth are "out" to their families. Recent studies have found that approximately 60%–70% of youth have disclosed their identities to at least one family member, and it has been noted that these percentages have shown an increasing trend over the past few decades (Cooper-Nicols & Bowleg, 2010; D'Augelli, Grossman, & Starks, 2008). The reactions received can include acceptance, respect, shock, disappointment, anger, rejection, and violence (Orban, 2003; Sadowski, Chow, & Scanlon, 2009), and are addressed in more detail in Chapter 10. About half of youth experience negative reactions when disclosing their identity to parents (D'Augelli et al., 2008). Rejected youth may face threats, verbal, physical, and sexual abuse, as well as complete rejection from their families. These negative reactions can lead to high rates of homelessness among LGBTQ students. Conflict in the home (e.g., parental refusal to accept identity, parental anger at identity, verbal abuse, physical abuse) due to a youth's identity is the primary cause of homelessless for this population (Ray, 2006). Exact rates of homelessness are difficult to identify, however there is a notable disproportionality regarding the percentage of homeless youth that are LGBTQ (5%–50% across studies) (Ray, 2006). Being homeless is an additional risk factor, as life on the streets may put any youth at risk of physical violence, drug use, or incarceration.

In some families, parents are supportive of their LGBTQ students. Additionally, some students may have some support from a few key family members, even if one parent is not supportive. However, it is important to remember the possibility of a supportive and positive reaction from parents or other family members. Also, immediate familial reactions may change over time, and even parents who were initially upset or angry may become supportive. For youth with supportive families, the home environment can function as a protective factor. For youth with unsupportive or rejecting families, the home environment is viewed as a source of risk.

School Context

Researchers have given much attention to the role of school climate in the lives of LGBTQ students. Unfortunately, much of this research tells us that schools are not perceived as supportive or even safe contexts for LGBTQ students. According to the 2009 National School Climate Survey (Kosciw, Greytak, Diaz, & Bartkiewicz, 2010), the majority of LGBTQ youth report of hearing negative uses of the word "gay" (e.g., that's so gay, no homo), as well as high rates of hearing slurs or other homophobic remarks (e.g., faggot) about LGBTQ individuals (89% and 72%, respectively). Even more alarming are the reports from students that they heard slurs or homophobic comments from school staff, and a large portion (40%) of students reported that school staff or faculty *never* intervened when they heard other students making derogatory remarks (Kosciw et al., 2010). The combination of these events sends messages that this language is acceptable, and it establishes a school climate that is not supportive of LGBTQ students. In addition to these tangible indicators of school climate, schools may have non-supportive climates due to what they are *not* doing. By not including LGBTQ individuals in the curriculum, not including protections for LGBTQ students in school policies, not supporting a GSA on campus, or not allowing sexual minority students to participate in events such as the prom, schools may be perpetuating heterosexist climates (Cooper-Nicols & Bowleg, 2010; Murdock & Bolch, 2005; Valenti, 2010).

The potential impacts of a negative school climate are vast. Negative climate is associated with feelings of isolation and a lack of safety at school, and it is highly correlated with skipping school, dropping out of school, and other negative school outcomes (Mayberry, 2006; McGuire et al., 2010). LGBTQ students found to be at the highest risk for negative outcomes are those who report negative school climates combined with low levels of personal support (e.g., peers, parents, teachers) (Murdock & Bolch, 2005). Also, a school climate that is not inclusive of LGBTQ students may prevent them from feeling a sense of connection or bonding with their school, thus eliminating a potential protective factor.

Many authors have noted that positive, safe, and supportive school climates can serve as protective factors for LGBTQ students, and research has identified several factors that contribute to this (e.g., Hansen, 2007; Orban, 2003). In their nationwide survey, Kosciw et al. (2009) reported that schools with large student bodies, lower student-to-teacher ratios, and higher percentages of college-educated adults were more likely to be perceived as safe contexts for LGBTQ students. Relationships with supportive school staff (regardless of sexual orientation or gender identity), including teachers, counselors, and GSA advisors were found to positively influence student perceptions of overall school climate as well as school safety (Murdock & Bolch, 2005; Sadowski et al., 2009; Valenti, 2010). Perceptions of school climate are positively impacted by the presence of a GSA or similar student club supportive of LGBTQ students (Cooper-Nicols & Bowleg, 2010). Even for youth who do not participate in a GSA, the presence of these groups on campus affects the entire school community in several ways, including increasing students' awareness of campus policies (students were more likely to be aware of inclusive anti-discrimination policies if there was a GSA on campus) (Hansen, 2007).

Maguire et al. (2010) found that a combination of school-related protective factors, including teacher intervention in instances of harassment, the inclusion of LGBTQ issues in the curriculum, and the presence of policies that protected students from discrimination or harassment based on sexual identity or gender expression predicted student perceptions of school safety. However, these authors also found that when students reported a positive relationship with at least one supportive adult on campus, these factors were no longer significant, suggesting that supportive relationships might be one of the most important aspects of school for LGBTQ students.

Peer Context

Interpersonal relationships are vital in the lives of all students. As with school and home climate, a student's peer group may either positively or negatively influence psychological well-being (Savin-Williams, 1994). Rates of harassment, bullying, and other victimization illuminate the fact that not all students are supportive of their LGBTQ peers. However, research also shows that LGBTQ and non-LGBTQ peers can function to protect LGBTQ students from the negative effects of victimization (Cooper-Nicols & Bowleg, 2010). These students often risk harassment themselves in order to support their LGBTQ peers, and may do so by simply being good, supportive friends or by participating in advocacy (Linville & Carlson, 2010). Some experts refer to heterosexual friends of LGBTQ students as *allies*, although students are not likely to use this term to describe themselves. Peer support may depend on disclosure of LGBTQ status: if students have not told any of their friends that they are LGBT or are questioning their identity, peers will not be in a position to help advocate for their friends (Orban, 2003).

Community Context

Schools exist within the broader social climate of the communities they serve. Attitudes, values, and fears (e.g., homophobia, biphobia) come from outside school walls as well as from within (Burns, 2007). In this way, community factors may influence the lives of LGBTQ students on a number of levels. In their nationwide survey, Kosciw et al. (2009) identified many community-level factors associated with school climate and victimization rates. One important factor was region: LGBTQ youth were more likely to be victims of harassment or discrimination if they lived in the South, and less likely if they lived in the West or Northeast. These differences were explained by factors unique to each region, such as the proportion of urban versus rural communities (urban communities were less associated with victimization), poverty rates, and the percentage of college-educated adults in the community. The connection of these factors to school-based risk and protective factors may be direct or indirect. For example, urban areas may be more likely to have large schools (school-based protective factor), and impoverished schools may not be able to afford teacher training on LGBTQ issues.

Socio-Political Context

The socio-political context impacts every other context in which LGBTQ students exist. Although the current socio-political climate regarding LGBTQ persons in the United States is challenging to dichotomize as either supportive or hindering, scholars researching LGBTQ issues describe the American social climate as heterosexist and either ignoring or largely unsupportive of this population (Burn, Kadlec, & Rexer, 2008; Larney, 2009). However, recent social phenomena suggest that representation and acceptance of LGBTQ persons in American culture appears to be slowly increasing, especially among younger generations (Savin-Williams, 2005).

In recent decades, there has been an increase in visibility and support of LGBTQ persons in mainstream culture. These increases may function as positive factors for LGBTQ youth. While in 1997 the main adult character on the television show *Ellen* (played by Ellen DeGeneres) coming out sparked social controversy, contemporary primetime television shows feature a number of lesbian, gay, and bisexual characters, including many shows about school-aged youth (e.g., *90210, Glee, Gossip Girl, Pretty Little Liars*) (Friedlander, 2011). Similarly, topics of gender identity have garnered attention on popular shows such as *Oprah* and *The Tyra Show*, which have featured transgender adolescents and adults. Interestingly, although LGBTQ individuals and characters have experienced more visibility in the media and entertainment industries, this trend has not been replicated in national sports. For example, there are currently no "out" male athletes in any of the top three sports in the United States (baseball, basketball, and football), and the very few prominent athletes from major sports that have come out as LGBT have done so after their playing careers ended (Stinson, 2011). However, there have been recent examples of professional athletes speaking out with their support of the LGBTQ community (e.g., NFL Player Michael Irvin appearing on the cover of *Out* Magazine, NBA player Steve Nash appearing in a video produced by the *Human Rights Campaign*). Additionally, former athletes and sports commentators (e.g., Charles Barkley and Bill Simmons) have discussed the fact that there *are* sexual minority athletes playing in high-profile professional sports (although identities have not been disclosed), and they speculated that a high-profile athlete would receive the support of his team if he did come out (Stinson, 2011).

The Internet provides another outlet for societal support of sexual minority students. As presented in Chapter 11, there is an incredibly rich variety of supportive and helpful information available for students, parents, and educators online. Students may utilize online sources to explore questions about sexual identity, gender expression, or the LGBTQ community in general. They may also find online supports such as chat rooms and blogs that connect them with youth experiencing similar thoughts, questions, feelings, and reactions. More recently, the Internet has been used as a gathering point for supportive individuals to come together and let LGBTQ students know that they are supported. In 2010, sadness over the widely publicized suicides of gay teens caused columnist Dan Savage and his partner to film and post a video online in which they spoke to LGBTQ youth with the message "It Gets Better." The video received widespread publicity and sparked a landslide of similar submissions. The resulting website, http://www.itgetsbetter.org, includes over 10,000 video messages, viewed over 35 million times, from thousands of adults, including athletes, politicians, and celebrities, all urging youth to have hope for their futures (Savage & Miller, 2011).

In contrast to increasing visibility and acceptance in the social climate, the political climate has been characterized by both advances and setbacks for the rights of LGBTQ individuals, making it more difficult to determine its potential impact on LGBTQ youth. The rights, privileges, and protections for the LGBTQ population have been hotly debated in American politics, and have resulted in nearly simultaneous advances and restrictions in the rights and protections for LGBTQ persons. These issues are politically divisive and have been compared to other divisive political and sociological issues such as desegregation of schools (Wald, Rienzo, & Button, 2002). LGBTQ issues have been targeted by political campaigns from the religious right (Larney, 2009), and phrases such as the "gay agenda" or "homosexual agenda" have been widely used by those who oppose representation or protection of LGBTQ persons in schools and in the larger society (Wald et al., 2002). It is not hard to imagine that the content of political campaigns arguing against LGBTQ rights could be perceived as negative messages about the LGBTQ community. For example, campaigns against gay marriage may present arguments that children and families are "better" if they are parented by a man and a woman. This argument may imply that LGBTQ parents are inferior, that children raised by LGBTQ parents have problems that children raised by heterosexual parents do not, etc. Stepping further back, consider the broader societal message being sent by the fact that in the current political climate, the rights of LGBTQ individuals are considered inappropriate items for voting or debate *at all*. Currently, it is impossible to imagine ballot measures or political campaigns regarding the rights and privileges of other minority groups, such as racial minorities or religious groups, but nearly every state has ongoing political turmoil regarding protections for and restrictions of LGBTQ persons. We cannot know the exact impact of these campaigns, debates, or the tumultuous political climate regarding LGBTQ rights on any given LGBTQ student, although logic implies that it is not yet a positive one.

Application to LGBTQ Students at Your School

The contexts in which LGBTQ students develop greatly influence academic, social, and mental health outcomes. Family, school, peer, and community factors can serve to support development, or can prove devastatingly unsupportive. All of these contexts exist within the larger socio-political context, which is in a near-constant state of change. A brief summary of the risk and protective factors for LGBTQ youth across contexts is included on the CD. Within this already complex dynamic, we must remember that all students, including all LGBTQ students, are unique individuals. Keeping this in mind, school professionals must accept that research cannot tell us how the various factors involved in the life of any one LGBTQ student have interacted to impact his or her development and well-being. For example, we cannot predict which protective factors may be most important for any particular student, or how important the presence of certain factors, such as supportive parents, teachers, or peers, may be in helping a student to overcome the risks he or she is exposed to in other contexts. Therefore, we must take what we know about potential risks and assets and use them as guidelines when we work with LGBTQ students. We know that students may be at risk for a number of negative outcomes, or may be exposed to negative experiences such as harassment or bullying, but we need to get to know each student as an individual before we can determine how, or even if, he or she requires our assistance to help develop into a healthy, successful young adult.

For educators, the take-home message regarding this extremely complex situation is that even small actions or influences *matter* in the lives of LGBTQ students. It matters how teachers relate to their LGBTQ students. It matters how school staff respond to anti-LGBTQ comments or bullying. It matters how peers treat their LGBTQ classmates. It matters how television shows are talked about at school. It matters how you vote. It matters what you do!

Four

Law and Policy in Action

Any school professional who aims to help create a supportive and responsive school environment for LGBTQ students must first understand the relevant laws and policies. The legal climate regarding LGBT rights in the United States is in near constant flux. As a result, even seemingly straightforward questions such as *"Is it illegal to discriminate based on sexual orientation?"* do not yet have definitive answers. Therefore, it is imperative that educators learn about the most recent case law, state regulations, and district policies that apply to the schools in which they work. This knowledge will help in two ways. First, it will help professionals at the school and district levels ensure that they comply fully with applicable laws and regulations. Second, it will help professionals to provide critical support to LGBTQ students seeking to understand their legal rights.

There are a few noteworthy legal cases regarding LGBTQ students and schools that illuminate both the extent of the problems (e.g., harassment, bullying, apathy of school employees regarding LGBTQ youth) and the potential consequences (e.g., legal fees, financial settlements, mandatory policy changes, and diversity training) for districts and administrators that allow these behaviors to continue unaddressed. Federal and state policies also affect the education of LGBTQ students and school practices. School personnel can use this information to adopt and implement policies at school and district levels that protect the rights of all the students they serve.

Examples of Cases Involving LGBTQ Students

The best known lawsuit involving an LGBTQ student is *Nabozny v. Podlesny*. Featured in the film *Bullied: A Student, a School, and a Case that Made History* (Teaching Tolerance, 2010), this case involved Jamie Nabozny, a student in Ashland, Wisconsin.

- Beginning in seventh grade, Jamie endured years of verbal and physical abuse from his classmates at school for being gay. The many bullying and harassment incidents outlined in the case included experiences such as being thrown to the ground and subjected to a mock rape in a science classroom, being assaulted then urinated on in a bathroom, and being beaten by a group of students to the point that he required abdominal surgery.
- Several times, Jamie and his parents met with school administrators and asked for support in protecting Jamie. Their complaints were dismissed and ignored; they were told that these behaviors were expected because Jamie was gay and that this type of bullying was normal because "boys will be boys" (Larney, 2009). Additionally, the identified attackers did not receive any consequences.
- In 1996, the court found three administrators (two principals and one vice-principal) guilty of discrimination in their failure to protect Jamie from other students. In contrast, the district itself was not found guilty, as there were clear policies stating that harassment on the basis of sexual orientation was prohibited.
- After the verdict, but before punitive damages were awarded, a settlement was reached requiring the district to pay Jamie nearly one million dollars.

The Fourteenth Amendment to the U.S. Constitution (discussed later in this chapter) guarantees the right of all citizens to equal protection under the law. The court held that the administrators who worked with Jamie did not provide him with equal protection, because if this harassment had happened to another (heterosexual) student, the consequences for the attackers and response in support of the victim would have been much different.

Another often cited case involving an LGBTQ student and a school district is *Henkle v. Gregory*. Derek Henkle was a high school student in Reno, Nevada who began to be harassed after speaking out about being gay on a local television show. Derek was repeatedly attacked at school, including one instance when attackers placed a lasso around his neck in a school parking lot and attempted to drag him behind a truck.

- As in the *Nabozny* case, school administrators took no actions against Derek's attackers. Instead, Derek was told by a school administrator that he needed to "stop acting like a fag" (Keen, 2007). In response to Derek's complaints, the school and district moved Derek from school to school (instead of dealing with the perpetrators in any fashion), eventually having Derek complete a GED instead of earning a diploma.

- In 2002, Derek's case against the district reached a pretrial settlement of $451,000. In addition, the district agreed to implement policies to protect future students from discrimination based on sexual orientation.

One of the most important aspects of this outcome is the implication that districts cannot tell students to not act "gay." Students have a right under the First Amendment of the Constitution (discussed later in this chapter) to speak about their sexual orientation and related issues in the school setting (Lambda Legal, 2000). Another important implication is that in this case, as with many others, the school district was not only forced to pay damages, but also to implement changes to protect future students.

A final example of a case involving LGBTQ students is *Flores v. Morgan Hill Unified School District*. Settled in 2004, this case involved Alana Flores (a student perceived by others to be a lesbian) and five co-plaintiffs (unnamed junior high and high school students experiencing anti-LGBTQ victimization) in Morgan Hill, California.

- Alana experienced years of anonymous verbal and written harassment at school, including threatening messages (e.g., "Die dyke bitch" and "We'll kill you") and violent pornographic material posted on her school locker (Larney, 2009).
- Her school did not investigate these messages, refused to change her locker, and left the messages up for several months before cleaning her locker.
- The district eventually settled and was required to pay over one million dollars in damages (to Alana and her five co-plaintiffs), as well as provide annual training to staff and anti-harassment programs for students, create and advertise new policies regarding complaint procedures, and assign a compliance coordinator for each school.

In this case, the appeals court found that the school district denied its students equal protection under the Fourteenth

Amendment, and showed "deliberate indifference" in its failure to investigate and take action against perpetrators of harassment (Esseks, 2010).

New cases involving LGBTQ students and schools are being brought to court every year. School districts have been found liable for (Ali, 2010; Esseks, 2009, 2010, 2011; Sun, 2010):

- Failing to respond to bullying and harassment;
- Preventing students from asserting their identity while participating in school functions (e.g., attending prom with a same-sex partner, dressing according to gender identity for yearbook photos);
- Preventing Gay-Straight Alliances (GSAs) or similar clubs from forming or meeting on campus;
- Blocking access to websites that have positive messages about the LGBTQ community;
- Violating students' privacy by disclosing their sexual orientation to parents.

In response to these findings, districts have been required to:

- Pay large monetary damages;
- Revise school policies and handbooks to protect LGBTQ students;
- Allow GSAs to meet;
- Allow students to bring same-sex dates to the prom;
- Provide diversity and LGBTQ-specific training to staff and students;
- Have compliance coordinators monitor their implementation of these requirements and report back to the courts.

Relevant Federal and State Law

Federal Law

Equal Protection Clause of the Fourteenth Amendment. One of the most common legal protections utilized in lawsuits protecting LGBTQ students is the Equal Protection Clause of the Fourteenth Amendment to the U.S. Constitution (§ 1983). The specific language within this amendment that is of interest is the section that lists what states can and cannot do to individual citizens, which reads "nor shall any State deprive any person of life, liberty, or property, without due process of the law; nor deny to any person within its jurisdiction the equal protection of the laws."

According to this clause, if a school district protects any student from harassment or discrimination, it must similarly protect *all* students (Keen, 2007). In cases such as *Nabozny v. Podlesny*, *Henkle v. Gregory*, and *Flores v. Morgan Hill Unified School District*, this is exactly what district employees failed to do. In these cases, as well as in many undocumented instances of bullying and harassment of LGBTQ students, district officials do not respond to anti-LGBTQ victimization in the same manner that they would harassment based on race, class, or other reasons. Many administrators dismiss acts of harassment toward LGBTQ students, sometimes due to their own negative beliefs about sexual minority individuals (Bedell, 2003).

District employees might be held liable for actions that violate the equal protection rights of LGBTQ students (as in the *Nabozny* case). The presence of a district policy on harassment or discrimination, including those discussed later in this chapter, does not impact the individual liability of district employees. For example, suppose that a school district has an anti-harassment policy that explicitly prohibits discrimination on the basis of sexual orientation. Further suppose that an LGBTQ student reports an incident of such discrimination to the vice principal. If no investigation is carried out and no actions are taken against perpetrators, the vice principal might be guilty of violating that student's right to equal protection (Bedell, 2003).

Title IX of the Educational Amendments of 1972. Some incidents involving LGBTQ students on school campuses might fall within the scope of Title IX of the Educational Amendments of 1972 (20 U.S.C. §1681). This federal law, commonly referred to as Title IX, states that "no person in the United States shall, on the basis of sex, be excluded from participation in, be denied the benefits of, or be subjected to discrimination under any educational program or activity receiving federal financial assistance." Title IX does not explicitly prohibit discrimination on the basis of sexual orientation, and many courts have failed to identify sexual orientation harassment as sexual discrimination according to Title IX (Bedell, 2003). However, Title IX does protect all students from sexual harassment (Esseks, 2010). Attacks such as those made against Alana Flores (*Flores v. Morgan Hill Unified School District*), in which the perpetrators used sexually explicit materials to harass, are

covered under this amendment. Title IX has also been successfully applied to protect students who have been harassed
for not conforming to sex or gender stereotypes (Keen, 2007).

The First Amendment. The First Amendment to the U.S.
Constitution protects freedom of speech. This freedom applies
to LGBTQ students in many ways. First, it protects the ability of LGBTQ students to freely express themselves as LGBTQ
individuals. Schools cannot ask students to hide their identity
or force students to wear clothing that matches their biological sex. This also means that students have the right to wear
the clothing of their choice to school-based functions and
events, such as the prom and their yearbook photos (American Civil Liberties Union [ACLU], 2011). Additionally, the
First Amendment prohibits schools from utilizing software
filtering systems that restrict access to websites that are supportive of LGBTQ individuals (Sun, 2010). The First Amendment also protects students who wear clothing that features
pro-LGBTQ statements or messages, or who make speeches
with similar content, with some restrictions. Schools may
prohibit language that is lewd, vulgar, obscene, or threatening (ACLU, 2006). Similarly, students may be prohibited from
freedom of expression if that expression interferes with the
rights of others or significantly disrupts classes (ACLU, 2006).
The CD contains letters to school administrators prepared by
the ACLU that address web filtering and censorship of LGBTQ
students.

Family Educational Rights and Privacy Act (FERPA). The
Family Educational Rights and Privacy Act (FERPA; 20 U.S.C.
§ 1232g) states that any educational institution that receives
federal funding must make student records available to parents for review (Keen, 2007). When considering LGBTQ students, FERPA may become an issue if students' records
contain any information regarding sexual orientation (e.g.,
membership in a GSA). In this case, parents or legal guardians
would have a right to review this information (upon request).
This could be problematic if students had not disclosed their
sexual orientation to their family, and especially if students
had a reason to expect a negative or hostile parental reaction
to this information.

Schools should be cautious when compiling educational
records in order to carefully respect students' right to privacy.
Students have the right to either share or withhold information regarding their sexual orientation or gender identity.
Moreover, it is illegal for schools to disclose this information,

even if students appear to share it freely in the school setting (Sun, 2010). The CD contains a letter to school administrators prepared by the ACLU that addresses student privacy.

Equal Access Act. In 1989, the Equal Access Act (EAA; U.S.C. § 4071) was passed. This act began as a statute written to allow religious groups to meet on public school campuses (Esseks, 2011). The EAA ensures that in junior high and high schools that receive federal funding, if any non-curricular student organizations are allowed to meet on school grounds, schools cannot deny access to the school for any particular non-curricular group, such as a Gay-Straight Alliance (GSA). Under EAA, access to a school refers to (Larney, 2009):

- The ability to use school space to hold meetings;
- Official recognition from the school regarding the existence of the club;
- Use of school methods for conveying notices or publications (e.g., newsletters, signs posted in the hallway, use of the school loudspeaker).

In spite of this protection, many districts have refused or delayed the formation of GSAs. For example, administrators in Salt Lake City, UT refused to allow a GSA to form in 1995 (Mayberry, 2006). In this case, the school district chose to eliminate all student organizations in order to prevent the GSA from forming (thus treating all non-curricular student groups "equally"). However, it was determined that the district did not actually ban all groups, and allowed some to continue meeting (*East High Gay Straight Alliance v. Board of Education of Salt Lake City School District*). In 2000, this case was voluntarily dismissed after the district allowed the GSA to meet. The EAA also prohibits school districts from utilizing software filtering systems that restrict student access to websites that provide supportive resources for LGBTQ students, as this would restrict a GSA from having the same resources and privileges available to other student groups (Sun, 2010).

In addition to strategies such as banning all student organizations, districts have tried other strategies to prevent the formation of GSAs. For example, districts have argued about morality, about the potential to discuss sex in a GSA, and about not wanting to "endorse homosexuality," and have required GSAs to change their names (Esseks, 2011). Lawsuits involving these actions have been decided in favor of GSAs (Esseks, 2011).

Other strategies have resulted in mixed responses from the courts (Whittaker, 2009). For example, some districts have created policies requiring parental permission for participation in extracurricular clubs. This may prevent students from participating in a GSA, particularly if students are not out to their parents or if parents are not supportive of an LGBTQ or ally identity. The CD contains a letter to school officials prepared by the ACLU that addresses EAA and the formation of GSAs.

State Law

Currently, the United States does not have federal laws that protect against discrimination, harassment, or bullying based on sexual orientation or gender expression. The laws and statutes identified earlier in this chapter have provided the legal basis for cases being settled in favor of LGBTQ students, but there are no explicit national laws that specify that it is illegal to allow students to be harassed based on sexual orientation or gender expression. However, our legal system allows states to create laws that provide individuals with more protections than are available via federal law, and several states have taken such measures to protect LGBTQ rights. For example, California has passed legislation (A.B. 9, 2011) that requires school districts to adopt inclusive anti-bullying and anti-discrimination policies. As state laws are subject to change, school professionals are urged to carefully examine the current laws regarding discrimination, bullying, and harassment in their state.

Table 4.1 contains a list of state laws and regulations that involve LGBTQ issues. The states and laws listed were retrieved from the Human Rights Campaign (www.hrc.org/state_laws) in 2011 (April 12, July 6, July 11). The Human Rights Campaign is a civil rights organization that advocates for the equal rights of LGBTQ persons. The first two laws addressed in Table 4.1 pertain to LGBTQ adults, specifically regarding marriage and the ability to jointly adopt children (i.e., the right to apply to adopt a child as a gay or lesbian couple rather than as an individual). The remaining laws and regulations are directly applicable to students in schools. As shown, 18 states (plus Washington, D.C.) specifically protect students from discrimination, harassment, and/or bullying based on sexual orientation (16 of these states protect based on sexual orientation *and* gender expression). Although these lists are accurate as of August 2011, it is important to remember that laws, especially

Table 4.1 Laws Involving LGBTQ Persons and Students by State

Law Type	Applicable States
Marriage for Same-Sex Couples	Connecticut, Iowa, Massachusetts, New Hampshire, New York, Vermont, and the District of Columbia
Joint Adoption for Same-Sex Couples	Arkansas, California, Colorado, Connecticut, Illinois, Indiana, Iowa, Maine, Massachusetts, Nevada, New Hampshire, New Jersey, New York, Oregon, Vermont, Washington, and the District of Columbia
Anti-Discrimination, Anti-Harassment, and/or Anti-Bullying Laws based on Students' Sexual Orientation and Gender Identity	Arkansas, California, Colorado, Connecticut, Illinois, Iowa, Maine, Maryland, Minnesota, New Hampshire, New Jersey, New York, North Carolina, Oregon, Vermont, Washington, and the District of Columbia
Anti-Discrimination, Anti-Harassment, and/or Anti-Bullying Laws based on Students' Sexual Orientation (without gender identity)	Massachusetts, Wisconsin
Anti-Discrimination, Anti-Harassment, and/or Anti-Bullying Laws for Students (no categories of protection listed)	Alabama, Alaska, Arizona, Delaware, Florida, Georgia, Kansas, Kentucky, Louisiana, Mississippi, Missouri, Nevada, North Dakota, Ohio, Oklahoma, Rhode Island, South Carolina, Tennessee, Texas, Virginia, West Virginia, and Wyoming
States with Regulations or Ethical Codes for Teachers that Address Discrimination, Harassment, or Bullying of LGBT Students	Hawaii, New Mexico, Pennsylvania, Utah

laws regarding LGBTQ individuals, may change rapidly. In order to ensure accurate information, school practitioners should stay abreast of the politics, elections, and changes in their state.

In addition to the specific state laws addressed here, the United States Department of Education's Office of Civil Rights released a statement in 2010 reminding school districts of their legal obligations to protect students from discrimination and harassment based on sexual orientation, gender expression, race, national origin, or disability (Ali, 2010). This release, in the form of a "Dear Colleague" letter, outlines the federal laws protecting student rights, provides examples of different types of discrimination, and provides suggestions regarding steps districts can take in order to ensure that they are in compliance with the law. Although this letter is not the equivalent of explicit legal protections for LGBTQ students nationwide, it is a sign that anti-LGBTQ harassment and bullying is being recognized as a serious problem by the U.S. government.

Review and Revision of District and School Policies

In addition to the protections granted by federal and state laws, school districts and individual schools may elect to include specific statements regarding bullying and harassment based on sexual orientation and gender expression in their policies. Such actions send a message to the entire school community that LGBTQ students are not going to be mistreated or marginalized (Szalacha, 2003). These policies state that the protection of all students on campus is a priority, and proclaim that actions targeting students based on sexual orientation or gender expression are not acceptable. In these ways, explicit policies support staff and students who are already intervening in cases of anti-LGBTQ harassment, and force school staff who are not already intervening to do so (Szalacha, 2003).

The adoption and consistent enforcement of school policies is the most recommended action for schools to take in order to eliminate bullying, harassment, and discrimination of LGBTQ students (Hansen, 2007). School or district policies do not replace state or federal laws, and students at schools without such policies are still entitled to similar protections. Instead, these policies are a proactive way for schools and districts to communicate the importance of preventing anti-LGBTQ bullying and harassment to the school community. Additionally, explicit policies help teachers and administrators to immediately recognize what behaviors require investigation and/or intervention, and ensure that students and concerned parents have been adequately informed about what types of behaviors will result in disciplinary actions.

The adoption of inclusive anti-bullying and anti-discrimination policies has been shown to significantly decrease the number of anti-LGBTQ behaviors on school campuses. Kosciw, Greytak, Diaz, and Bartkiewcz (2010) examined differences in various types of victimization of LGBTQ students in schools with no policies addressing harassment or bullying, schools with generic policies (i.e., did not specify sexual orientation or gender identity), and schools with inclusive policies. In schools with inclusive policies, staff intervened in about one-quarter of incidents involving biased remarks against LGBTQ students, compared to about 16% in schools with generic policies and only 10% in schools with no policies. Similarly, students reported that staff intervention was effective when they reported incidents of discrimination over 40% of the time in schools with inclusive polices, compared to 36% of the time in schools with generic policies, and 29% of the time in schools with no policies. These results highlight the efficacy of this relatively simple intervention in helping to create safe school environments for LGBTQ students.

Content of Inclusive Bullying and Harassment Policies

When reviewing a school's current policies, school professionals should look for language that clearly identifies what behaviors constitute bullying and harassment as well what groups are identified for protection. In specifying groups, districts should explicitly mention *actual or perceived* sexual orientation and gender expression in order to ensure that students who do not identify as LGBTQ, but are harassed or otherwise victimized as if they were LGBTQ, are still protected. In addition to identifying what *must not* be done, policies should clearly specify what *should* be done. Policies should address requirements and procedures for reporting bullying and harassment (most policies have mandated reporting requirements for staff), and clearly identify what actions the school will take upon receiving a report of bullying or harassment (e.g., immediate investigation and disciplinary actions) (Kosciw & Diaz, 2008). Policies should also reflect and/or reference a school or district's overall mission statement to include, welcome, and support all students and families.

Many examples of model school policies are available for school professionals to review online. Websites of organizations such as the ACLU and the National Center for Lesbian Rights have posted model inclusive anti-bullying and anti-harassment policies, and several states have posted similar model policies via their department of education, state teachers' union, or state association of school boards' websites (e.g., Colorado Association of School Boards, Michigan Department of Education, New Jersey Department of Education). School administrators should work with leadership teams to review their own policies, examine extant model policies, and propose changes or modifications accordingly.

It is also important that districts consider policies that protect staff and faculty. Research has indicated that employees are more likely to be open about an LGBTQ identity, or to be actively involved as an ally for LGBTQ students when they have tenure, due to concerns over losing their jobs as retribution for these actions (Savin-Williams, 1994; Valenti, 2010). As relationships with supportive and caring adults at school has been identified as a strong protective factor for LGBTQ students (discussed in Chapter 3), school districts should remove the potential barriers to these relationships by creating policies that protect employees in these situations.

Enforcement of School Policies

Regardless of the policies that a district has in place, students are not truly protected unless these policies are widely known and consistently enforced. Sadly, studies have demonstrated that many districts do not enforce their protection policies as written, or do so only intermittently. Non-enforcement or inconsistent enforcement defeats the purpose of these policies, both by denying some students the direct benefit of action and by signaling to all concerned that non-discrimination is viewed as a low priority. Consistent implementation is needed to ensure that students are adequately protected (Cooper-Nicols & Bowleg, 2010; Watson, Varjas, Meyers, & Graybill, 2010).

In order to ensure consistent enforcement, administrators need to be clear on how to respond to instances of harassment and bullying. Without established protocols, inconsistency in enforcement is unavoidable. There are no clear guidelines regarding what actions districts should take to respond to perpetrators of violence and discrimination. Districts and administrative teams should decide on the consequences they believe are appropriate, keeping in mind that disciplinary actions need to be coupled with education for perpetrators. Some perpetrators may not understand why their actions were wrong (Cooper-Nicols & Bowleg, 2010), and therefore may require an explanation in addition to disciplinary action. These protocols and guidelines should be the same regardless of the type of harassment or bullying (e.g., racist comments, sexual harassment).

One of the most important steps that districts can take toward consistent enforcement of inclusive school policies is to ensure that the entire school community is aware of their existence (Hansen, 2007). Sadly, in many districts that have taken the time to revise their policies to protect LGBTQ youth, large portions of the student body are unaware of these changes (Szalacha, 2003). Awareness of policies on the part of students, staff, parents, and administrators gives visibility to the protection of LGBTQ students on campus, and helps to increase accountability regarding consistent enforcement. Schools may discuss policy changes in school newsletters, hold parent meetings, review policies with staff, and educate students about school policies during orientation or similar events.

Working with School Boards

Often, changes in school policy must be approved by the school board. Therefore, it is important that any school professional desiring to implement this type of change is knowledgeable regarding the district's process for proposing materials before the school board (e.g., notification, early submission of materials, scheduling). The Gay-Straight Alliance Network, Transgender Law Center, and the National Center for Lesbian Rights (2004) propose the following strategies for working with school boards to implement LGBTQ-inclusive anti-bullying and harassment policies:

1. Bring a supportive group to the school board meeting that represents all levels of the school community (i.e., teachers, administrators, parents, students);
2. Prepare all arguments and materials in advance;
3. Provide relevant research and statistics regarding the prevalence of anti-LGBTQ bullying and harassment, as well as the potentially positive impacts of implementing an inclusive policy;
4. Take notes on board members' questions and votes for follow-up;
5. Regardless of immediate vote outcome, send all board members follow up messages thanking them for considering the policy.

These organizations also recommend that if policies are not adopted immediately, that the policy development team review the outcome of the meeting and strategize to eliminate the obstacles for the next presentation.

A Call to Action

Putting aside the moral and ethical reasons for creating respon-sive and inclusive schools where all students can learn in a safe, supportive environment, federal and state laws (a brief review of applicable laws is included on the CD), along with legal precedent, are sending a clear message to district and school personnel: LGBTQ students have the right to expres-sion, the right to expect equitable treatment, and the right to be educated without harassment or bullying. Regardless of educators' personal beliefs or feelings, they must take appro-priate and meaningful action when instances of discrimina-tion and bullying are brought to their attention.

Case Studies

Sydney

After this incident, the school psychologist asked Mr. Green to come to campus for a follow-up meeting. He did not want to pressure Sydney's father to disclose information about his family that he was not ready to share, but he wanted to convey to Mr. Green that he and his family were all welcome members of the school community. He assured Mr. Green that Sydney was an important member of their school's community, and that the school was eager to work together with all members of her family in order to see to her best interests. He also referred to the school's mission statement, which explicitly stated that all families were an important part of education at their school. He expressed his concern that Sydney had become upset at school when she had called the "wrong person," and suggested that it may help if Mr. Green chose to provide the school with current information regarding any parental fig-ures in Sydney's life, in order to ensure that the school has all of the best ways to reach her family should any needs or emergencies occur.

Mr. Green told the school psychologist that he was hesi-tant to discuss his family because they had met a great deal of resistance at Sydney's previous school. Her first grade teacher had told Sydney that she needed to keep her "Uncle Matthew" a secret from her classmates. When Mr. Green and his part-ner came to the school to discuss the incident, the principal had told them that she agreed with the teacher's position, because it was not appropriate to talk about sex in a first grade classroom. After they moved to a new district, Mr. Green and Mr. Homer (Matthew) had decided it was best to not disclose their relationship to Sydney's new school, as she was so upset and hurt by her previous teacher's reaction.

The school psychologist reminded Mr. Green that it was his choice if he wanted to disclose his family constellation to the school community, and assured him that he would respect his and his partner's right to privacy should they elect not to discuss their family with the school. He also offered to attend any meetings that Mr. Green wished to have with the school's administration or Sydney's teacher in order to ensure that all parties understand that Sydney and her family are welcome members of the school community. At the end of the meeting, Mr. Green told the school psychologist that he and his partner would discuss the situation and contact him when they reached a decision.

Jessie

Jessie's parents are rightfully concerned about the lack of support they received regarding Jessie's safety at school. After they made the decision to homeschool Jessie, they contacted an attorney to ask a few questions regarding their experiences with Jessie's middle school. The attorney informed them that, in California, there are laws that protect students from discrimination, bullying, and harassment based on sexual orientation and gender identity. Also, Jessie has a constitutional right to be herself at school (i.e., First Amendment), and therefore she cannot be told to "act like a boy." Additionally, case law has established that districts need to appropriately investigate incidents of bullying and harassment. As Jessie's parents have heard from other families that incidents of bullying or harassment involving non-transgender students have been quickly and thoroughly addressed, the district may have violated Jessie's Fourteenth Amendment right to equal protection. After this meeting, Jessie's parents decided to file a lawsuit against the district.

Before the meeting with Jessie's parents, the administration at the high school reviews district records for Jessie. The principal notices the multiple complaints filed by Jessie's parents regarding discrimination and harassment. At the meeting, the principal and school psychologist work with Jessie's parents to create a plan to keep Jessie safe at her new school. First, the administrative team reviews the anti-bullying and anti-harassment policies in place at the high school, helping Jessie's parents to understand that mistreatment based on Jessie's gender expression will not be tolerated. Jessie's parents are optimistic about the high school after this initial meeting, and appreciate that the administration was so proactive in helping them to understand the rules in place to protect Jessie, as well as the steps that will be taken should they or Jessie report a problem.

Five

Developing Awareness and Sensitivity

LGBTQ Issues in the School Community

In order for schools to be responsive to LGBTQ students and families, LGBTQ issues need to be addressed at both the staff and student levels. Educating staff, administrators, and other key stakeholders in the school community about LGBTQ issues is a critical step that schools must take, and this is often a necessary foundation before teachers begin developing inclusive classrooms (Chapter 6) or consistently implementing and enforcing bullying and harassment prevention strategies (Chapter 7). Similarly, students need exposure to LGBTQ issues, information about school policies, and explicit expectations for treatment of all students in school. Appropriate professional development activities for school staff and diversity training for students can positively impact the school climate for LGBTQ students and families, as well as create an overall tone where all students feel safe and supported. These school-wide activities work best when couched within the framework of school policy and administrative practices that clearly address respect for and protection of LGBTQ students and families (which are addressed in greater detail in Chapter 4).

School Staff

Staff Training

It is widely accepted that diversity is an important topic to address during pre-service training programs for future teachers, administrators, and school-based mental health professionals, but it is unclear to what extent, if any, LGBTQ issues are specifically covered. Experts agree that the majority of school professionals, including administrators, school psychologists, school counselors, and teachers are not adequately trained in their graduate training programs in how to support LGBTQ youth (Goodrich & Luke, 2009; Graybill, Varjas, Meyers, & Watson, 2009), and that the majority of teachers-in-training have slight to strong negative opinions of sexual minority individuals (Morgan, 2003). Not surprisingly given the lack of pre-service training, research has shown that few teachers are knowledgeable about LGBTQ populations (Morgan, 2003). This lack of education and understanding may explain the rates of LGBTQ students reporting that teachers fail to intervene in instances of harassment, blame victims of harassment, make homophobic remarks in school settings, and harass LGBTQ students (Gastic & Johnson, 2009; Holmes & Cahill, 2004; Kosciw, Greytak, Diaz, & Bartkiewicz, 2010; McGuire, Anderson, Toomey, & Russell, 2010; Watson, Varjas, Meyers, & Graybill, 2010). Clearly, training in LGBTQ issues is not systematic or adequate; thus school staff will need professional development training to understand the unique challenges experienced by LGBTQ students and families and to learn how best to create responsive school environments.

When planning for staff development, it is important to keep several points in mind. First, a two-hour workshop is not enough to make a large impact on behaviors or beliefs. It can be an important first step, perhaps helping staff to recognize personal biases or values regarding diversity (Koerner & Hulsebosch, 1996). Second, staff turnover is a reality in the school system, more in some areas than others. Therefore, staff development related to LGBTQ issues must be viewed as a long-term commitment. Workshops, meetings, or in-service trainings should be scheduled as a series and conducted at least annually, so that school staff, both old and new, are kept up to date about this important information (Cooper-Nicols & Bowleg, 2010; Szalacha, 2003).

Assessing School Needs

Before creating any diversity or LGBTQ-specific training materials, it is important that trainers fully understand the needs at a particular school site or across the district. A needs assessment is a formal or informal process that gathers information about the knowledge base, concerns, questions, and perceived problems of the intended audience for professional development activities. A thorough understanding of the types of factors that can help or hinder development in LGBTQ youth will help guide school professionals in understanding the types of information that will be useful to gather. A brief review of risk and protective factors is included on the CD (with materials for Chapter 3).

Trainers can create surveys, including questions about participants' familiarity with the risks faced by LGBTQ students, familiarity with laws and policies protecting LGBTQ students from discrimination and harassment, observations of harassment or bullying of LGBTQ students on campus, their comfort level with addressing LGBTQ issues in their classrooms, and their understanding of the needs of LGBTQ parents and their children. Informally, the needs of a school's staff may be apparent by reviewing reports of student and parental concerns regarding LGBTQ harassment or discrimination or by holding information-gathering meetings with LGBTQ students, Gay-Straight Alliance (GSA) participants, or parents. If schools have gathered broad information about a school's needs for the purposes of planning bullying prevention programs (discussed in Chapter 7), then a separate needs assessment for the purposes of planning staff development may not be necessary.

Trainer Competence

When thinking about a professional development program to educate school staff about topics related to LGBTQ students and families, it is critical to ensure that the person providing the training has adequate knowledge about working with LGBTQ individuals. There may be someone on the school staff with the background knowledge to provide the training, such as the school counselor or school psychologist. However, as the aforementioned research suggests, even school-based mental health professionals may not have received adequate coursework on this topic in their programs. Thus, it may be necessary for that person to acquire additional professional development (e.g., attending a workshop at a professional conference) before they have the knowledge and skills to provide staff professional development (Whitman, Horn, & Boyd, 2007).

Alternatively, schools can bring in an expert facilitator to provide professional development activities on LGBTQ issues. One option for this is the Gay, Lesbian, and Straight Education Network (GLSEN), which trains facilitators to provide professional development activities in schools at a relatively low cost (J. Betz, personal communication, August 16, 2011). Schools can get more information about GLSEN's services by contacting the national organization or local chapters (http://www.glsen.org/cgi-bin/iowa/all/about/locations/index.html).

Adult Professional Development

After ensuring that the person providing the training is competent, it is important to consider how to present information in a way that will be most effective with adult learners (i.e., school staff). At the beginning of the training, it can be helpful to establish a common starting point for all present (Knowles, Holton, & Swanson, 2005). This might be done through a handout given to school staff ahead of time about the experiences of LGBTQ students, a warm-up activity (such as the Impact of Silence Activity on the accompanying CD), a video clip, or having each person, including the trainer, respond verbally to a prompt such as, "I became an educator because _____." The trainer can ask participants about their reactions to what they have read or seen or can highlight common themes from what participants have shared. Next, the trainer should clearly state the purpose of the training, with a focus on why it is important (Knowles et al., 2005). For example, the trainer might say, "LGBTQ students often experience intense bullying and harassment at school, and today, we are going to talk about concrete steps you can take to address this in your classrooms." It is also helpful to present an outline of what will be covered in the training with clear learning objectives (Knowles et al., 2005).

Good professional development programs employ a variety of instructional methods to engage school staff with the material they are learning. Thus trainers should consider using a combination of the following techniques (Gilley, 2004; Rogers & Horrocks, 2010):

- Lecture to provide background and content (e.g., defining terms such as "homophobia");
- Demonstration to model techniques (e.g., how to respond to a derogatory remark);
- Small-group work to facilitate discussions;
- Role-playing to allow participants to practice what they are learning;

- Case studies to allow participants to apply what they are learning in new ways and address obstacles.

At the end of the training, it is helpful to engage participants in a whole-group discussion to tie everything together, answer final questions, and encourage participants to try out their new learning with students (Knowles et al., 2005).

Professional Development Programs

In general, professional development programs should focus on three points: evaluation of personal and institutional beliefs and biases; information about LGBTQ issues such as bullying and discrimination; and education about strategies, practices, and behaviors to create supportive school environments. Throughout the trainings, but especially when exploring personal biases and values, it is important to develop a climate of safety to encourage open and honest participation.

The first goal of professional development is to help school staff clarify "their own values, attitudes and experiences" (Young & Mendez, 2003, p. 18) surrounding sexual orientation, gender identity, and harassment of LGBTQ individuals. Exercises to help with values clarification can include questions such as:

- "What is my definition of a family?" (Koerner & Hulsebosch, 1996, p. 350);
- "What have been my experiences with gay men and lesbian women?" (Koerner & Hulsebosch, 1996, p. 350);
- "Do the examples I use in class assume that everyone is heterosexual?" (Mathison, 1998, p. 153);
- "Have I ever said anything in or out of class that would let the students know how I feel about homosexuality?" (Mathison, 1998, p. 153).

When exploring values, it is important to discuss heterosexism and the messages, both hidden and explicit, that the school as a whole and individual staff members are portraying to students (Koerner & Hulsebosch, 1996). Concepts such as heterosexual privilege, the often overlooked privileges enjoyed by heterosexual individuals that are not shared by sexual minorities (such as holding hands with a significant other in public without judgment from others), can be strong discussion points.

The second goal of professional development is to provide accurate information about LGBTQ youth and families. This might include reviewing terminology, presenting facts about identity development and the range of sexual and gender identities and behaviors found in youth, and presenting information about harassment, bullying, and the challenges particular to LGBTQ students. This information may help school staff understand the importance of the training, recognize the necessity of intervening in cases of mistreatment among students, and correct any myths or misinformation regarding homosexuality.

The final and ultimate goal of professional development is to prepare staff to implement strategies that can make their classrooms and other school environments more responsive, supportive, and welcoming of all youth and families. This might include strategies to include and support LGBTQ students and families and sample lesson plans to teach students about general diversity and LGBTQ sensitivity issues. It is critical that trainings involve discussions, case studies, and role-plays regarding responding to harassment to ensure that school staff know how to respond when this occurs (Young & Mendez, 2003). Chapter 6 provides information on classroom climate and integrating LGBTQ issues into curriculum, and Chapter 7 provides information about school climate, bullying, and harassment.

A number of professional development resources and programs exist that are appropriate for use with school staff. While programs may need to be modified or adapted to meet the specific needs of the school population, they provide a good starting point for planning professional development activities.

Understanding and Supporting Lesbian, Gay, Bisexual, and Transgender Youth (Russell, nd). This is a day-long training program designed to educate school personnel about sexual orientation and gender issues. The curriculum covers relevant terminology, risk and resiliency factors, developmental outcomes, the coming out process, and awareness of personal values. The Lesson Plan for this curriculum is provided on the accompanying CD. Professionals can obtain a free copy of all the materials necessary for the training, including a training manual and PowerPoint, by contacting Dr. Russell at strussell@arizona.edu.

Stand Up for Us: Challenging Homophobia in Schools (Jennett, 2004). This guide provides resources for educators working in elementary and secondary schools with the goals of helping educators appropriately recognize and respond to homophobia and create more inclusive, safer school environments to meet the needs of all students. This guide offers suggestions for how to keep track of homophobic events in the school setting, how to challenge and respond to homophobic events, and how to support students who disclose their sexual orientation at school. A list of resources and materials is provided that support the activities and strategies outlined in the guide. The guide can be retrieved from the following site: http://www.nice.org.uk/niceMedia/documents/stand_up_for_us.pdf.

Welcoming Schools: An Inclusive Approach to Addressing Family Diversity, Gender Stereotyping, and Name-Calling in K-5 Learning Environments (Human Rights Campaign Foundation, 2009). This program is designed to be used in elementary schools to improve school climate for LGBT parents and their children, to increase involvement by LGBT parents to support academic achievement, and to incorporate LGBT topics into general discussions of diversity around campus. The program addresses three main topics: family diversity and strategies for school staff to welcome diverse students and families; gender stereotyping and strategies to support students who do not conform to traditional gender roles and stereotypes; and systemic change to reduce name calling and bullying. Preliminary research suggests that by using the information provided in the program, educators reported a positive impact on school diversity climate and felt less concerned about their knowledge of and ability to work with LGBT parents and their children. Lesson plans from the Welcoming Schools program are provided on the CD. The program guide can be retrieved from the following site: http://www.hrc.org/documents/An_Introduction_to_Welcoming_Schools.pdf.

Beyond the Binary: A Tool Kit for Gender Identity Activism in Schools (Gay-Straight Alliance Network, Transgender Law Center, & National Center for Lesbian Rights, 2004). This resource includes an outline of a training to educate school staff about transgender and gender non-conforming students, with information on legal issues, gender identity development, challenges encountered by these students at school, and scenarios. This resource is available on the CD or from the following site: http://www.gsanetwork.org/get-involved/change-your-school/campaigns/beyond-binary.

Students

Like school staff, students need a clear understanding of school policies and expectations regarding the treatment of all students, including those who identify as LGBTQ and those who others perceive to be LGBTQ. Research suggests that even heterosexual students who do not engage in bullying their LGBTQ peers often still display indicators of prejudice, such as not wanting to be friends with LGBTQ students (Poteat, Espelage, & Koenig, 2009). While school staff's actions will greatly influence the overall school climate, students will also benefit from school-wide programs to increase their awareness of and sensitivity to diversity issues, including both overt bullying and more subtle forms of prejudice and discrimination toward LGBTQ students (Poteat et al., 2009).

Peer-Led Education

As students move from elementary school to middle school (and for some, from early to late elementary school), peers have an increasing amount of influence. Overall, research suggests that peer-led prevention and intervention programs, or at least programs that have peer-led components, are as beneficial, if not more beneficial, than programs that are led solely by adults (Cuijpers, 2002; Mason, 2003; Mellanby, Newcombe, Rees, & Tripp, 2001; Valente et al., 2007). When peer leaders are carefully selected, educational programs can capitalize on social influence, role modeling, and accessibility to positively influence peers' beliefs, attitudes, and behaviors (Cuijpers, 2002; Mason, 2003; Valente et al., 2007). Although this research is not specific to programming to increase sensitivity to LGBTQ issues, it is likely that the factors that make peer-led programs effective will hold true for this topic.

Diversity Programming

School-wide diversity programming will likely look different depending on the population of the school and needs of the students and community. Similar to developing professional development for staff, a needs assessment can help guide programming for students. Diversity programs do not need to focus solely on LGBTQ issues, but this topic should be explicitly addressed as part of the program (Fisher et al., 2008).

Bauman and Sachs-Kapp (1998) provide an example of a school-wide program to promote diversity that included an LGBTQ component. In an effort to promote tolerance of diversity, a series of workshops focusing on the theme, "Hate Hurts," were conducted for the student body on topics such as racism, gender equity, religious differences, and sexual orientation. The workshops were facilitated by student leaders who were recruited by and received approximately 100 hours of training from school counselors. The training included activities to increase self-awareness, to develop effective group facilitation skills, to identify guest speakers on specific diversity topics, to practice running groups, and to practice scripts to assist with workshop delivery.

Bauman and Sachs-Kapp (1998) provide a basic outline of the day-long workshop to educate students about issues for sexual minority individuals:

- A guest speaker with expertise in high-risk youth and drop-out prevention spoke to the entire student body.
- In smaller groups, students rotated through three panels moderated by student leaders that included:
  - A high school student talking about his experiences as a young gay man;
  - Family members of LGB individuals talking about how they are impacted by derogatory comments and discrimination;
  - Professional psychologists talking about the effects of discrimination and hatred.
- In groups of about 10 students each, students were encouraged by student leaders to process their feelings and thoughts about what they had heard that day.
- The workshop concluded with an activity for the entire student body on how "hate hurts."

Bauman and Sachs-Kapp (1998) reported that there were some negative responses when the workshop was first publicized at the school. The school administrator took decisive action, addressing the issue at the all-school convocation. Additionally, students were allowed to choose to attend an alternative workshop instead that focused on general themes of fear and intolerance (only 8 students out of 150 chose this alternative).

Building Support and Managing Resistance

School board members and other high level district officials (e.g., superintendents) should not be excluded from education efforts regarding LGBTQ students and families (Goodrich & Luke, 2009; Szalacha, 2003). Given the large influence these individuals can have on school activities, policies, and climates, these individuals/groups can be in a position to either help or hurt school climate for LGBTQ students and families (Watson et al., 2010). Thus, it may be necessary to educate administrators, board members, and other decision makers, and to seek their support before trainings can be offered to school staff or students. While providing education about LGBTQ issues might include some of the content covered under "Professional Development Programs" in this chapter, it is recommended that training for school board members or other high level school administrators contain up-to-date legal information as well (which is addressed in Chapter 4).

Change takes time and patience, and this may be especially true when working in schools. As with any system involving so many people, it is expected that some individuals will resist the implementation of new policies, paradigms, or programs. Initiatives to increase visibility, safety, and support of LGBTQ students and families will likely meet resistance from some contingent in the school community. This contingent could represent those in power, including those who are formally in positions of power (e.g., superintendents or school board members) or those who are informally in positions of power (e.g., senior staff members, influential parents). This means that resistance on the part of a small number of individuals could have a large impact on the success of a program or initiative (Jeltova & Fish, 2005). The degree of resistance will vary greatly depending upon several factors, such as the broader social and political climate of the surrounding community. In order to work through resistance, one needs to understand who it is coming from, as well as why those individuals are resistant (Jeltova & Fish, 2005). Resistance to diversity or awareness training is often associated with misconceptions or myths about the LGBTQ population and is best addressed through education. Teaching resistant participants the dangers of not protecting LGBTQ students is one recommended strategy (Cooper-Nicols & Bowleg, 2010; Graybill et al., 2009). Another strategy is to remind resistant individuals that their moral obligations as educators (e.g., to enhance the well-being of all students) outweigh personal beliefs they have about sexual orientation, gender expression, or family constellations (Koerner & Hulsebosch, 1996).

Case Study

Jessie

After the initial meeting with Jessie's parents, the high school principal continues developing a plan to make the school environment welcoming for Jessie. Although the school has had annual staff trainings on general issues of diversity and bullying/harassment prevention, the principal feels that it would be beneficial to all if this year's training provided staff with more specific information on supporting transgender students. She finds the *Beyond the Binary* program, and she and the school psychologist review the suggestions from that training guide and begin to plan for the fall staff workshop. She begins the process of searching for a guest speaker who can complement the planned activities for the training program.

In addition to the staff workshop, the school principal wants to provide some information on gender diversity to the student body. The school psychologist suggests that they work with the student government association, such that the student body leaders may receive training regarding gender diversity and then create their own ways to deliver this information to their peers. The principal has a meeting with the student body president and student government staff advisor, who are supportive of the idea. The student government had hosted activities for the *Day of Silence* in the past, and the president is eager to work toward future efforts to make the campus a safe place for all students.

Six

Creating Diverse and Responsive Classrooms

Over the span of their careers, many teachers will never know how many LGBTQ students they have taught or how many of their students have LGBTQ family members. Therefore, creating diverse and responsive classrooms cannot wait until teachers *know* that they have a gay student or a student with LGBTQ parents. The guiding principles for creating diverse and responsive classrooms must be present all the time. Teachers that celebrate diversity and demand that all individuals be treated with respect will make a positive impact on all students.

Teachers should "have a vision of how their classroom practices influence or shape students' development" (Hollins, 1999, p. 15). This is important because teachers' actions, or lack of action, can validate and engage students or can perpetuate prejudice and discrimination (Hollins, 1999). By taking a thoughtful and informed approach to developing classroom climate and by making curriculum choices that honor diversity, teachers can create classrooms that are more responsive to LGBTQ students and families.

Classroom Climate

Teachers' Influence

As discussed in Chapter 3, research suggests that teachers have a significant impact on the school experiences of sexual minority students. Sexual minority students with positive views of their teachers are less likely than those with negative views to experience school problems (Russell, Seif, & Truong, 2001), and those who report more support from teachers have a greater sense of psychological belonging, even when other aspects of the school climate are less than ideal (Murdock & Bolch, 2005). Similarly, the school experiences of LGBTQ parents and their children can be positively or negatively affected by the classroom climate.

General Strategies

To begin creating more diverse and responsive classrooms, teachers should:

- Practice using the terms *gay, lesbian, bisexual, transgender,* and *questioning,*" and use them naturally in context to reduce the stigma associated with the words (Daniel, 2007);
- Practice responding to student questions about LGBTQ terminology or LGBTQ individuals;
- Display LGBTQ posters, stickers, books, and pictures of diverse family constellations (Daniel, 2007; Mufioz-Plaza, Quinn, & Rounds, 2002). (Sample posters are available on the CD in the materials for Chapter 8.)

Teachers should also take advantage of "teachable moments," when students bring up LGBTQ content at unexpected times (Bryan, 2010; Daniel, 2007). Bryan (2010) suggests doing this by taking a stance of curiosity and asking students what they know or understand about the topic. She gives the example of a small group of third grade students talking about giving out valentines, and one student commenting that boys giving other boys valentines is "gay." In this instance, the teacher might use open-ended questions to find out what the students understand and how they came to this understanding. Bryan (2010) gives these examples: "How come it's okay for girls to send friends a valentine and not for boys?" "Who made that rule?" "Did everyone get to vote?" (p. 47). Students need to have these kinds of conversations with adults repeatedly during their school years, as students will interact with the issues differently at different developmental stages (Bryan, 2010).

Classroom Rules and Addressing Derogatory Comments

Classroom rules focused on expectations of respect for all students are an appropriate foundation for building a safe and accepting classroom climate. The wording of the rules will vary depending on students' developmental level, but the message is the same. Additionally, teachers need to make clear that they will not tolerate any derogatory remarks, put-downs, or slurs (Daniel, 2007). Comments that imply negative feelings about sexuality and gender, such as "That's so gay," "Don't be such a girl," and "No homo," must be attended to immediately. It is suggested that teachers respond to all comments to send a clear message, and teachers can use these moments as an opportunity to teach students about the meaning of the words and the disrespectful nature of the comments. If comments continue, teachers can let students know that there will be more severe consequences if they continue to use disrespectful language. Teachers must be consistent in enforcing these classroom rules so students understand the expectations for respecting diversity in all its forms.

Responsive Curriculum

Much has been written about creating curriculum that is responsive to the needs of diverse students, although most of the focus has been on curriculum for racial, ethnic, cultural, and linguistic diversity. However, the principles that guide the development of responsive curriculum at both the elementary and secondary levels hold true and can be easily extrapolated to the inclusion of LGBTQ students and families into the curriculum.

Guiding Principles

Curriculum can both explicitly and implicitly impact student learning. Explicit curriculum teaches students things like facts and dates (e.g., presidents and multiplication), while implicit curriculum teaches students how certain people and things are viewed or valued within society (e.g., social power and perceptions of majority versus minority cultures) (Shropshire, 1999). It is from implicit curriculum that students learn social roles and expectations (Shropshire, 1999). When groups such as LGBTQ persons are left out of explicit and implicit curriculum, schools may be sending the message to LGBTQ students and their classmates that LGBTQ individuals are not valued or equal in society. Responsive curriculum is designed to validate "the experiences of all students, with particular attention to students ... whose histories and stories have been overwhelmingly excluded from classroom study" (Athanases, 1999, p. 139).

Teachers can help create responsive curriculum by infusing content reflecting people from a range of diverse backgrounds (Athanases, 1999). However, it takes time and effort for teachers to do research, read new books, and develop new lessons. Developing curriculum that is more responsive to LGBTQ students and families takes a commitment and intentionality from teachers, and may require teachers to reflect on their values, prejudices, and discomforts (Athanases, 1999). Additionally, a truly integrated curriculum focuses on diversity all the time, not only on a special day, week, or month.

It cannot be ignored that curriculum that integrates LGBTQ issues may be controversial. Engaging students in dialogue about topics such as sexism, racism, homophobia, and oppression, whether in a history class discussion about the Holocaust or in an English class discussion about censorship and persecution of authors such as Oscar Wilde, may bring up feelings of anger, frustration, or sadness for students. Many students will relate to experiences of prejudice and discrimination even if they do not identify as LGBTQ, and it is these commonalities that can help to form the basis for a productive dialogue. In order to encourage students to grapple with these situations, ideas, and feelings, teachers need to both value this type of learning opportunity and provide structure for students to engage in these conversations so that all students feel heard and empowered to effect change. If teachers fail to create a climate where these types of conversations are encouraged and valued, some students may feel disengaged, disrespected, and disheartened.

Reading/English/Literature

English curriculum is an ideal place to integrate works by and about LGBTQ people. Books help to weave diversity into curriculum, and they are one of the primary ways that students explore the world in which they live. Books can help affirm and validate students' identities and teach about the lives of other students (Perkins, 1999). Students who see aspects of themselves in books are more likely to be engaged and construct meaning from what they are reading (Perkins, 1999). Also, students who learn from books about those who are different from themselves or their families may be better prepared to accept diverse people when they encounter them in life.

The books available in a classroom, both those read to students and read by students, send a message about who is valued in school and in society (Perkins, 1999). Selecting texts for class and books for a classroom library is one of the most important steps a teacher can take in creating responsive curriculum. However, it has been suggested that teachers generally choose familiar books, often those based on literature they experienced in their own homes and schools (Athanases, 1999). Thus, teachers committed to developing responsive curriculum for LGBTQ students and families may require resources to help them identify and access appropriate classroom materials. Identifying these materials at the elementary and secondary levels is an important step to take in developing inclusive curriculum.

Elementary School. There are two goals for LGBTQ responsive curriculum in elementary school. The first is to recognize and validate LGBTQ-headed families and their children. The second is to create an environment that lays a positive foundation for students' current and later sexuality and gender identity development. These goals are not mutually exclusive, and activities to meet the first goal will also serve the second, and vice versa.

An important consideration when introducing LGBTQ curriculum for elementary students is their cognitive development. In early elementary school, students' ability to think and reason is very concrete. For many students, this concrete reasoning extends through later elementary school as well (and for some, into middle school). An awareness of this cognitive stage allows teachers to present curriculum in a manner that students are capable of understanding. For some students, the concepts of *gay*, *lesbian*, *bisexual*, and *transgender* may simply be too complex or abstract. This does not mean that these concepts are ignored; rather, teachers should simply recognize that some students may not understand them. Instead of focusing on these concepts, it is recommended that elementary school teachers provide repeated exposure to family diversity. As discussed previously, this exposure, as well as all other curricular recommendations included in this chapter, should occur within a safe classroom climate.

Books are an excellent way to introduce family diversity. For young children with parents who are LGBTQ, understanding their role in their family provides a positive sense of belonging, and children's books featuring sexual minority (primarily gay or lesbian) characters can be used as tools in early elementary grades (Chick, 2008). Such books serve two functions: to validate the experiences of students from LGBTQ-parented homes, and to teach other students that families that are different from their own in this aspect are similar in nearly every other way. Chick (2008) suggests the following books for Kindergarten through second grade teachers to include in their curriculum and classroom libraries to address family diversity:

- *The Family Book* (Parr, 2003) and *All Families Are Different* (Gordon, 2000) address how families are alike and different, with sexual minority headed families among the many different types of families discussed.
- *Antonio's Card (La Tarjeta de Antonio)* (Gonzalez, 2005) is written in both English and Spanish and presents the ways in which a young boy who lives with his mother and her partner manages teasing at school.
- *Molly's Family* (Garden, 2004) is about a Kindergarten girl with two moms who is trying to understand her family structure as compared to that of the other students.
- *My Two Uncles* (Vigna, 1995) addresses a girl's confusion when her favorite uncle and his partner are excluded from a family celebration.
- *King & King* (de Haan & Nijland, 2000) and *King & King & Family* (de Haan & Nijland, 2004) are about a prince who falls in love with and marries a prince (*King & King*) and then they decide to adopt a baby together (*King & King & Family*).
- *And Tango Makes Three* (Richardson & Parnell, 2005) tells the true story of two male penguins who build a nest together and care for an egg (and subsequent baby penguin) from another penguin couple who laid an extra egg.
- *Best Best Colors (Los Mejores Colores)* (Hoffman, 1999) is about colors and diversity and features a boy with two mothers.

Depending on the developmental level of students, many of the aforementioned books are appropriate for students beyond second grade, and teachers in later elementary school can continue to include them in the curriculum and classroom library.

There are two important considerations when including books with gay and lesbian characters at this age level and beyond. First, LGBTQ issues are not solely about sex, and books on these topics focus on a range of developmental and social issues (Walling, 2003). Second, the experiences highlighted in these books are appropriate for all students, as books are a way that students learn about the lives of people both similar to and different from themselves (Walling, 2003). Teachers do not teach books about African Americans only to the African American students in class or books featuring female lead characters only to the girls in class. Books recommended for students at this developmental level allow students to see themselves in the characters and to be exposed to realities that might be quite different from their own (Walling, 2003).

Schall and Kauffmann (2003) provide an example of a lesson implemented with fourth and fifth graders that was designed to investigate students' knowledge about gay and lesbian issues and their reactions to books that included gay and lesbian characters. First, the topic was introduced by the teacher. She asked how many students heard another student being called "gay" and allowed students to share their ideas of what "gay" meant, probing for clearer definitions of the word. Next, the teacher asked the students where they learned about what it meant to be gay. After this, the teacher read aloud *King & King* (de Haan & Nijland, 2000), allowing students to share their initial impressions after the beginning of the story, ideas and observations about the text and illustrations throughout the story, and reactions to the end of the story when the prince falls in love with another prince. After the story was completed, students were encouraged to discuss whether or not they thought the story was appropriate for children. The teacher then asked how many students felt bothered by the book (with about half the class responding in the affirmative), and the teacher told the class that they could choose books to read with other themes if they liked. The teacher then allowed students to choose books to read (alone, in pairs, or in small groups), including a number of books with gay and lesbian characters. All but five students chose to read these books. After students were given time to read several books, the teacher divided the class into small groups to discuss what they had read. During the discussion groups, students were allowed to talk freely.

During the small-group discussions, Schall and Kauffmann (2003) report that students expressed a wide range of feelings and ideas about the books, and several themes emerged. Many students expressed confusion about some of the ideas brought up in the books, but stated a desire to understand different kinds of relationships (viewing homosexuality as different but not wrong). Students expressed a desire to have accurate information about gay and lesbian people and their children, but felt unsure if it was okay to talk about these topics outside of the classroom activity (e.g., with family members). Overall, the authors report that the students were quite curious about the topic but lacked accurate information.

The aforementioned example tells educators that students are using the word "gay" in a derogatory way early on and are confused about what it means to be gay. Students in this developmental stage generally want information so that they can form meaning about what they are learning inside and outside of the classroom. Students who are not ready to talk about this topic (e.g., the five students who chose other books to read) should not be forced to do so (Schall & Kauffmann, 2003). However, creating an open environment and starting the conversation early allows students to begin to recognize the legitimacy of sexual and gender diversity.

It should be noted that texts highlighted in this section focus on gay and lesbian characters, as there are few books that cover bisexual, transgender, and questioning identities at the elementary level. Additionally, while these topics are certainly valid for inclusion in curriculum, as can be seen from the example above, even fourth and fifth grade students may not have the capacity to understand these more complex concepts. As students move into middle school, they are cognitively more capable of managing these multifaceted constructs.

Middle and High School.   Middle and high school students, many of whom are in the throes of puberty, can begin to understand the shades of gray that exist when talking about sexuality and gender identity. At this developmental level, it is appropriate to include more substantive curriculum on LGBTQ issues, and to continually push students just beyond their comfort zones so they are encouraged to use their prior knowledge to understand increasingly complex and abstract ideas.

Many books in middle and high school English and literature classes explore themes of love, sex, and family. It is appropriate to broaden these topics to be inclusive of LGBTQ relationships (Greenbaum, 1994). Although there are a few books that teachers can include in the curriculum that center on LGB characters (as will be discussed below), many commonly used middle and high school English texts can introduce sexual and gender diversity through discussions of subtext (Greenbaum, 1994). Subtext can highlight a number of issues worthy of discussion, such as sexism and racism, and teachers should not shy away from also helping students recognize explicit and subtle references to homosexuality, bisexuality, and gender diversity (Greenbaum, 1994).

Greenbaum (1994) highlights a number of commonly used texts that would be appropriate to explore in terms of characters' LGBQ sexuality or sexual encounters, including:

- Celie's lesbian relationship in *The Color Purple* (Walker, 1982);
- Brick's possible homosexuality and Big Daddy's homophobia in *Cat on a Hot Tin Roof* (Williams, 1954);
- Holden going to Mr. Antonelli's house in *Catcher in the Rye* (Salinger, 1945);
- The possibility of Tom being gay in *Glass Menagerie* (Williams, 1945);
- Homoerotic subtext in Shakespeare's *Julius Caesar*.

A number of books on LGBTQ topics are appropriate for students in middle school and high school, and teachers will need to make selections based on the developmental and reading levels of their students. Walling (2003) suggests books with gay and lesbian characters, as well as those questioning their sexuality, that may be appropriate for middle and high school students:

- *If It Doesn't Kill You* (Bechard, 1999) is about a ninth grade boy struggling to come to terms with his father's disclosure that he is gay.
- *The Year They Burned the Books* (Garden, 1999) is centered on a high school senior trying to understand the controversy over the school's new sex education curriculum that includes information on sexual minority individuals while she is trying to understand her own sexuality.
- *Holly's Secret* (Garden, 2000) is about a girl adopted by lesbian mothers who creates a new identity for herself and her family upon moving to a new town.
- *Name Me Nobody* (Yamanaka, 2000) deals with many life issues, including parental abandonment, weight and dieting, and sexuality.

- *The Blue Lawn* (Taylor, 1994) is set in New Zealand and tells the story of two teen boys discovering that they are gay.

Szymanski (2010) suggests several books appropriate for teens that have characters exploring the range of sexuality, including bisexuality and questioning:

- *Split Screen: Attack of the Soul-Sucking Brain Zombies/ Bride of the Soul-Sucking Brain Zombies* (Hartinger, 2007) is the same story told from the perspective of a gay adolescent and from the perspective of his best friend Min, who is attracted to both boys and girls.
- *Empress of the World* (S. Ryan, 2001) is about a girl attending a girls' school trying to understand her feelings for her best friend.
- *Ash* (Lo, 2009) showcases a main character who experiences attractions to both a male and a female character.

Transgender issues are more difficult to find in the literature, but a book appropriate for high school students that might start a discussion about this topic is *As Nature Made Him: The Boy Who was Raised as a Girl* (Colapinto, 2000). This true story chronicles the lives of twin boys, one of whom was raised as a girl after a botched circumcision. Although the book is not about a transgender individual, it does introduce issues about gender, biology, and environment that could easily frame discussions about gender identity and transgender.

Athanases (1996) provides an example of a gay-themed lesson for tenth graders that was part of a course titled, "The Ethnic Experience in Literature." After beginning the unit with a chapter from a Martin Luther King, Jr. book, the teacher decided to include the essay *Dear Anita: Late Night Thoughts of an Irish Catholic Homosexual* (McNaught, 1988). The essay is addressed to Anita Bryant, who campaigned against allowing gay people to teach school during the 1970s. Across the course, the teacher hoped to engage students in explorations of differences and similarities, to help them develop sensitivity to diversity and marginalized groups, including gay and lesbian people, and to help them recognize commonalities among people experiencing racism, sexism, homophobia, and other forms of discrimination and oppression.

Athanases (1996) reports that the "Dear Anita" lesson began by assigning students the essay to read as homework after providing them with some background about Anita Bryant's campaign. The following day, students discussed the essay in class and were directed to write a response that addressed each of the author's major points and analyzed how well he addressed Anita Bryant's concerns. At the end of the unit, students took a quiz that included the question: "If Martin Luther King were to express his view on the plight of gay people as mentioned in the 'Dear Anita' article, what might he say, based on what you know if his philosophy?" (pp. 237–238).

Athanases (1996) analyzed the lesson using audio and video recordings of the class discussion, interviews with the teacher and a sample of students in the class, and analysis of student essays and quiz responses. He describes the teacher's role in the class discussion as being a facilitator, starting the discussion by having students talk about the author's culture and religion as a backdrop to the experiences he highlights in his essay. Throughout the discussion, the teacher asked questions and made comments, but generally let the students lead the discussion and respond to each other without a great deal of teacher input. In terms of the discussion, topics that were raised included a gay person's right to be a teacher, whether or not homosexuality was a choice, myths about homosexuality that were addressed in the essay, children raised by lesbian or gay parents (this was not addressed in the essay but many students had opinions about this topic), and the possibility of someone in the classroom being gay or lesbian and how he or she would feel about the students' discussion.

Athanases' (1996) analysis of the students' writing related to this lesson revealed several themes. First, the lesson helped students to recognize myths and stereotypes they held about gay men and move beyond them. Two stereotypes that came up frequently were that gay men were child molesters and gay men were promiscuous and focused on sex. Students shared ideas from the reading and personal experiences that dispelled these myths. Second, the lesson helped students develop empathy for gay and lesbian people. Students seemed particularly affected by the author's suicide attempt, and some expressed feelings of guilt for the prejudices they held towards gays and lesbians. The third theme that emerged focused on equity and justice. Generally, students expressed that they felt gay men deserved equality and that Martin Luther King Jr., would support acceptance of and rights for all people. A fourth theme focused on identification and validation, with students identifying with the author's plight. The final theme focused on resistance to the acceptance of gays and lesbians. Work from two students indicated strong religious beliefs that being gay was wrong, and these beliefs were not impacted by the lesson.

From this example, the evidence is strong that even one lesson focused on gay and lesbian issues can make a difference and provide an opportunity for students to learn about, or at least question, their assumptions and prejudices. Imagine the impact if lessons like these were infused throughout middle and high school curriculums for all students.

History/Social Studies/Civics

History texts have received much criticism for failing to portray diverse perspectives of historical events and for lacking adequate coverage of the experiences and influences of ethnic and cultural minorities, women, and LGBT individuals (Shropshire, 1999). In July, 2011, California became the first state to require that gay and lesbian history be taught in public schools, and, with this, comes the need for texts and curriculum reflecting the experiences and contributions of this group (Lovett, 2011). Coverage of LGBTQ issues, or issues of other traditionally underrepresented groups, should be integrated throughout the curriculum, rather than relegated to an inserted box on the side of a page or only discussed during a special week or month (Fisher & Thomas, 2009).

In integrating diversity into history curriculum, teachers can use the existing text as a starting point, helping students to critically examine what has been included and what has been excluded from the text (Shropshire, 1999). For example, lessons on some civil rights movements might be included in the text, but students can do research on movements that have been excluded (i.e., gay rights movement).

Another strategy is to connect with community resources and community members with knowledge of specific events to talk about different versions of history (Shropshire, 1999). Continuing with the example above, teachers might arrange for a series of speakers to come in to talk about their involvement with different movements, highlighting their personal experiences and sharing what it means to them to not be adequately represented in historical texts.

After activities designed to help students think critically about historical perspectives, teachers can facilitate discussions focused on questions such as (Shropshire, 1999):

- From whose viewpoint was the text written?
- Whose viewpoint was left out?
- In what ways do these viewpoints contradict each other?
- Are there reasons why particular viewpoints were left out?

Teachers might also help students understand what message this sends to students about who has value, and who does not have value, and how they can combat this message.

Additionally, LGBTQ issues can easily be raised during class discussions of current events. Current events provide a natural opportunity for learning and teaching, and in-class discussions can allow adolescents to critically examine their world in a safe and supportive setting. Some ideas for this include:

- Political battles over gay marriage in the United States and in other countries;
- Controversy over Chaz Bono on *Dancing with the Stars* in 2011;
- Social backlash for television shows such as *Glee*;
- Teen suicides resulting from bullying and harassment.

Teachers might also show news clips or bring articles to promote discussions on LGBTQ issues.

Sex Education

When sex education is inclusive of all sexual and gender identities and addresses all sexual health behaviors, it can positively impact LGBTQ students' development (Blake et al., 2001; Maurer, 2009). Appropriate sex education curriculum should be "accurate, useful, and nonjudgmental" (Maurer, 2009, p. 364). Also, it should integrate LGBTQ issues throughout the content rather than restricted to one section or unit.

Maurer (2009) provides some suggestions for responsive sex education. First, all sexual orientations should be discussed, using the words gay, lesbian, bisexual, and heterosexual (as well as other respectful terms). Students can be encouraged to think about how the term *sexual orientation*, which applies to heterosexual, homosexual, and bisexual individuals, came to be most associated with those who are *not* heterosexual. This marginalization is similar to how we often use terms to define those who are different from the majority culture, setting the majority culture as the norm. Second, teachers can correctly define and distinguish between sexual orientation and gender identity, being careful to only include the "T" of transgender when topics actually refer to gender identity (rather than just tacking it on to LGBQ). These are confusing concepts that might need revisiting throughout the curriculum. Third, teachers should address bisexuality as a distinct sexual identity, addressing myths and misinformation, and soliciting student perceptions of bisexuality. For example, consider the following questions: How is bisexuality portrayed in the media? Is bisexuality viewed as a transient identity on the way to being gay or lesbian? Fourth, teachers can intentionally weave examples of people in different types of relationships throughout the curriculum in discussions of dating, sex, and commitment. Finally, teachers can help students relate to the experiences of LGBTQ people by examining sexual and gender discrimination, prejudice, and bias as related to other kinds of oppression, as well as highlighting models of happy, successful LGBTQ individuals.

Additionally, it is critical that sex education addresses risky sexual behaviors. This need not focus solely on LGBTQ students, but it should explicitly address them. Responsive sex education provides LGBTQ-sensitive instruction (Blake et al., 2001), addressing topics such as safer sex for all combinations of partners, including information about preventing sexually transmitted infections and HIV, dangers of using drugs and hormones not prescribed by doctors, accessing health care, and factors that can inhibit LGBTQ individuals from talking openly to health care providers (Maurer, 2009). Pregnancy can also be discussed as research shows that lesbian adolescents are at high risk for teenage pregnancy (Maurer, 2009).

Science

Science offers teachers opportunities to be inclusive of LGBTQ issues in both indirect and direct ways. In science, students often learn about genetics and the importance of diversity as it relates to strengthening a species. By focusing on the ways that diversity naturally occurs across species, teachers can send an indirect message that diversity is a positive, desirable quality.

At the secondary level, science teachers can be more direct in their approach. For example, researchers are continually looking at genetic and other biological variations as related to human development. Science teachers might have groups of students examine the research on genetic/biological influences versus environmental/social influences (i.e., nature versus nurture) in the development of constructs such as intelligence, autism, sexual orientation, and gender identity. Also, teachers can discuss how constructs such as sex are more complicated in nature than the simple binary categories we initially learn. This conversation could include intersex individuals as an example of the types of genetic variations that exist in nature.

Science teachers can also include information on scientists who are LGBTQ, or scientific discoveries that might have significant impact on the LGBTQ community. For example, teachers might talk about breakthroughs in AIDS research, once considered a "gay disease" but now found among many different populations.

Math

Math may not inherently lend itself to inclusion of diversity, but words, even those used in math, are power. Math teachers and math texts have added diversity in the names, pictures, and concepts used in examples and word problems. Similar approaches can help make math more inclusive of LGBTQ individuals. For example, a word problem might start, "Mary and Lucia earn a combined income of $84,500" or "Julio and Marco are planning a special night out at the movies." Teachers do not need to explicitly point out examples that are more inclusive of LGBTQ individuals, as the purpose of these kinds of examples is to ensure that curriculum and examples used in schools are accurate representations of the world students experience outside of the classroom. Math teachers can also consider LGBTQ diversity as a lens through which data and statistics are presented. For example, teachers can present lessons that teach students to critically examine statistics and how they can be presented in different ways to support or refute a particular theory, such as research on children from LGBTQ-headed families.

Integrating LGBTQ in the common lexicon of classroom instruction and curricular content can go a long way to promoting inclusion and embracing diversity.

Contributions of LGBTQ Individuals

In addition to including LGBTQ issues in the curriculum, responsive curriculum highlights the contributions made by

LGBT individuals (Daniel, 2007). Usually, teacher-written or student-researched biographies include information about the individual's personal life, and sexual orientation/gender identity can be discussed as one aspect of the person. Several websites offer information about famous and influential LGBT people. The following are examples of relevant biography projects (http://www.lambda.org/famous.htm):

- A bulletin board on influential athletes might include Billie Jean King and Greg Louganis;
- Reports on famous artists/musicians might include Tchaikovsky and Frida Kahlo;
- Presentations on influential leaders and politicians might include Alexander the Great and Harvey Milk.

As students increase their understanding of the contributions of LGBTQ individuals, myths and stereotypes will be challenged and students will move toward greater acceptance of sexual and gender diversity.

Taking First Steps

The inclusion of LGBTQ issues should be as seamless as possible. By discussing LGBTQ individuals throughout the curriculum, as opposed to in separate units, educators create classrooms that reflect the diversity that exists outside of the classroom. Additionally, they can reinforce the message to all students that being LGBTQ is simply a part of an individual's greater identity. This message is vital to the establishment of safe school climates for all students.

It can take years to develop fully inclusive curricula. As new lessons, strategies, and approaches take time to develop, we suggest that teachers start with one small change. Introduce one new lesson, include one new book, or include more diverse names and scenarios when giving examples in class. Be intentional in creating an inclusive climate and curriculum. It is with these small changes that school professionals will build classrooms that respect and reflect all students and all people.

Case Studies

Sarah

At Sarah's parents' request, Mr. Martin talks with Sarah's teachers. Overall, the reports are positive. Sarah is outgoing and engaged in her classes, earning mostly A's. Sarah's social studies teacher comments that Sarah is quite the advocate in class, often bringing up issues of discrimination and oppression. She invites Mr. Martin to observe her class the next day when several students, including Sarah, will be sharing a current events project with the class.

Mr. Martin sits in on Sarah's social studies class. Sarah is the third to share her project, which focuses on same-sex marriage. She highlights the political campaigns occurring in several states and compares gay rights to the civil rights movement. Students then ask Sarah questions or make comments about her presentation. One student comments that Sarah is "always talking about discrimination," and to this Sarah responds, "Well, I'm just giving a voice to people who don't always have a voice." After class, Sarah's social studies teacher tells Mr. Martin that Sarah is quite well informed about social justice issues and debates well with other students in class.

Jessie

As the start of the school year approaches, the school principal calls a meeting with Jessie's teachers to discuss ways that they can all work together to ensure that Jessie is safe and welcomed in her classes. The principal knows from her own research regarding school climate and safety for LGBTQ students that representation of gender diversity throughout the curriculum is one of the best ways that the school can support Jessie. However, some of her teachers, especially her algebra and biology teachers, mention that they were unsure of how to accomplish this in their subjects. The principal and school psychologist provided suggestions such as utilizing inclusive language and avoiding gender assumptions or gender stereotypes as a place for these teachers to start.

In addition to proactive measures such as using inclusive gender terms and including representations of transgender individuals when possible, the principal reminds teachers that the way that they address any negative language or comments they hear about Jessie in their classrooms will set the example for all students. A few teachers mention that they are not sure how to address these comments in the moment, and are concerned that they might accidentally say or do the wrong thing. The principal takes note of this, and asks the school psychologist to include ideas and practice for intervening in instances of verbal harassment, put-downs, or name calling in the upcoming staff training workshop.

Seven

Ensuring Safe Schools
Preventing Harassment and Bullying

All students have a right to be safe at school. Viewed through this lens, it is difficult to understand the high rates of harassment and bullying that exist for LGBTQ students. As discussed in Chapter 3, anti-gay slurs, verbal harassment, threats, social exclusion, and physical harassment are the reality for many LGBTQ students in U.S. schools. These actions contribute to the higher rates of depression, anxiety, substance abuse, truancy, and school failure for sexual minority students. Given the potentially deleterious effects of harassment and discrimination, and the legal rights of LGBTQ students to a safe school environment (see Chapter 4), it is a priority for schools to eliminate bullying and harassment and to promote safe school climates for all students.

The strategies and programs discussed in this chapter are not intended to be stand-alone measures to prevent bullying and harassment, but instead are part of a comprehensive approach to improving school climate for LGBTQ students. For successful implementation to occur, schools need to take other actions, including:

- Creation and consistent implementation of appropriate policies (Chapter 4);
- Ongoing staff development and diversity training for students (Chapter 5);
- Increasing visibility of LGBTQ issues and people in curriculum (Chapter 6).

In fact, bullying prevention programming should only be undertaken once a school has committed to each of these aspects. When these conditions are in place, schools can take the necessary steps to create safe school climates for all students, in place of those that foster or tolerate discrimination, bullying, or harassment.

Bullying and Harassment in Schools

A myriad of behaviors and intentions are included in the terms *bullying* and *harassment*, as highlighted by the many definitions that exist for each of them. In general, bullying is a verbal, physical, or psychological behavior that is intended to cause harm or distress, is ongoing, and involves an imbalance of power among the participants. Harassment is behavior that is intended to harm, disturb, or upset another person.

In the years after the shootings at Columbine High School, there has been increasing focus on the prevention of bullying, harassment, and school violence. Via this surge of attention, school personnel have learned about the types of bullying and harassment that occur on school campuses, the roles of various students in these behaviors (i.e., bully, bystander, and victim), and the negative outcomes associated with bullying and harassment. There have also been many developments with regard to assessing school climate, staff education, policy development, and evidence-based intervention and prevention programs. Sample school-wide bullying and harassment programs include:

- Bully Busters (Newman-Carlson, Horne, & Bartolomucci, 2000);
- The Bully Free Classroom (Beane, 2005);
- The PREPARE Curriculum (Goldstein, 1999);
- Second Step (Committee for Children, 2010);
- Steps to Respect (Committee for Children, 2001).

However, the majority of this research and these materials do not specifically address the victimization of LGBTQ students (Horn, Kosciw, & Russell, 2009; Larney, 2009). In fact, none of these programs alone is sufficient to address homophobia, biphobia, or transphobia present on many school campuses, and must be used in conjunction with other specific efforts to address anti-LGBTQ beliefs, thoughts, and values.

Convening a School-Wide Bullying Prevention Team

Planning, implementing, and evaluating a comprehensive school-wide bullying prevention program is a very large task. Therefore, no school professional should take singular responsibility. Instead, a team of school professionals and other constituents should work together at all stages. School personnel, such as counselors and psychologists, are likely members of such a team, as their professions include training on needs assessment, program evaluation, and group leadership. It is also critical that the team involve members who are familiar with LGBTQ issues, such as a Gay-Straight Alliance (GSA) advisor or representative from a local LGBT agency. Equally important is the involvement of those who are formally and informally in power in a school, such as the principal, Parent–Teacher Association (PTA) president, or an influential, tenured teacher (Jeltova & Fish, 2005). Individuals such as these may be vital to successful implementation of any changes, so their inclusion in the decision making process is beneficial to all. As the planning team meets in the initial stages of the creation of anti-bullying and anti-harassment programs, several questions should be addressed, including (Jeltova & Fish, 2005):

- What are the needs at our school?
- What types of supports and programs are feasible for us to implement?
- Who can or will be involved?
- How will we know if it has made an impact?

Understanding the School's Needs

Before introducing programming aimed at improving the safety of LGBTQ students, information should be gathered about general bullying occurring on campus and actions directed specifically at this population. Several indicators are important to examine. Draughn, Elkins, and Roy (2002) provide a list of issues to cover during a needs assessment focusing on LGBTQ student safety:

- Resources that are currently in place on campus to support LGBTQ students;
- Prevalence of bullying;

- Types of bullying and victimization occurring (e.g., anti-LGBTQ slurs, physical attacks on LGBTQ students, cyberbullying);
- Locations where bullying occurs (e.g., classroom, hallways, bathrooms);
- Types of responses to incidents (e.g., no response, detention, lecture).

As with the needs assessments for diversity training programming discussed in Chapter 5, this can be achieved via informal and formal means. It is important that information be gathered from all potential sources, including students, teachers, support staff, administrators, and parents. Informal methods may include observations made by staff, administers or other key individuals (e.g., GSA advisors or leaders) or by reviewing discipline records or other documentation of harassment or bullying. Formal methods may include focus groups and surveys.

Several existing surveys may be helpful for determining the needs at a given school. One example is the *School Climate Assessment* (n.d.) provided by the Welcoming Schools Program (described in Chapters 5 and 9). This assessment is designed for use with elementary school staff, and is available on the Welcoming Schools website (www.welcomingschools.org). The topics covered in this tool include:

- Policies and administrative support;
- School-sponsored trainings and workshops;
- School climate;
- Teaching practices and resources;
- Personal comfort level;
- School and community issues.

Another useful survey, *Student Survey: Name Calling and Verbal Bullying* (GLSEN, 2004) was created to accompany the No Name Calling Week program. This survey contains 25 items that address bullying and harassment, including types of incidents (verbal, physical, social isolation), locations, frequencies, and perpetrators. It is available on the No Name Calling Week website (www.nonamecallingweek.org). The Safe Schools Coalition created *The School Climate Survey* (n.d.), a 16-item measure for students in grades 6–12 to assess harassment, bullying, resources, supports, school climate, and student perceptions of campus safety.

Implementing Programs

When implementing any bullying or harassment prevention program, it is important that all members of the school community are fully educated about it. Bullying or harassment can occur anywhere and at any time on a school campus. Therefore, it is important that all adults on campus (e.g., teachers, administrators, counselors, social workers, coaches, security staff, custodial staff, bus drivers, and teacher's aides) be aware of all policies, strategies, and interventions that are in place. It is also important that parents and students be informed of any programs or new policies being implemented.

Several bullying prevention programs include ready-to-use classroom activities and lessons, requiring teachers to be active agents in program implementation. Fidelity of program implementation (i.e., how closely the teacher adheres to the lesson plan) can greatly impact program efficacy. Similarly, generalization of skills and concepts introduced during bullying curriculum, including teacher reinforcement of observed social skills and teacher intervention as directed by the curriculum, have been found to result in a larger reduction in bullying and victimization behavior (Hirschstein, Edstrom, Frey, Snell, & MacKenzie, 2007). The planning team should keep these factors in mind when supporting the implementation of an anti-bullying program, and take necessary steps to ensure that teachers are trained to maintain fidelity and reinforce learned skills and behaviors outside of the intervention lessons.

Because verbal harassment is the most common form of victimization experienced by LGBTQ students in schools (Cooper-Nicols & Bowleg, 2010; Murdock & Bolch, 2005), and because it is correlated with physical harassment (Kosciw, Greytak, & Diaz, 2009), teachers and other school staff need training on how to address verbal harassment and anti-gay slurs both inside and outside of the classroom (which is also discussed in Chapter 6). Additionally, LGBTQ students report that they often hear teachers using negative language about LGBTQ individuals and that teachers fail to intervene when other students do so (Gastic & Johnson, 2009). These comments, and especially their acceptance or use by adults, create school climates that accept unequal treatment of LGBTQ students. In contrast, when these words or phrases are immediately corrected and eventually eliminated, school climates are positively impacted.

Some staff might require training regarding how to identify verbal harassment. For example, some teachers may fail to
intervene if they hear students use the phrase "that's so gay,"
because they are unaware that this phrase is derogatory. Other
staff may be unaware of what types of responses are appropriate. In these cases, trainers, GSA advisors, or members of
the anti-bullying leadership team can lead activities in which
school staff learn different strategies for responding to verbal
harassment and role-play interactions in order to learn which
styles and strategies work best for them. Suggested strategies for teachers to utilize in addressing comments such as
"that's so gay" might include direct education (e.g., "that is
offensive because …") or mild humor (e.g., "is it possible that
it is straight?") (Graybill, Varjas, Meyers, & Watson, 2009). For
cases of direct harassment, staff should be educated regarding
school policy and the importance of immediate and consistent
intervention.

Key Aspects of Bullying Prevention Programs

In order to address these issues across the student body, it
is important to teach all students what types of actions and
behaviors are considered bullying or harassment. This is
typically one of the primary goals in the beginning stages
of a prevention program (e.g., Beane, 2005; Newman-Carlson
et al., 2000). These programs also teach students the roles
of bullies, victims, and bystanders, and address things that
each group can do in order to stop the cycle of bullying on
campus. For example, because an audience of bystanders is
often reinforcing to a bully, interventions teach students
that their responsibility is to discourage (address the bully
if safe or immediately report the incident to an adult) rather
than laugh, stare, or whisper, which may encourage bullying
behaviors. Finally, most bullying prevention programs
include social skills education. These lessons focus on bullies,
victims, or all students, and typically address skills such as
effective communication, empathy, respect, self-esteem, anger
management, and managing conflicts.

Addressing Cyberbullying

Cyberbullying is the use of technology to harm another person (Bauman, 2011). The flourish of readily available technology has increased the ways in which a student can be

cyberbullied, including chatrooms, instant messaging (IM), blogs, social media sites (e.g., www.facebook.com), texting, and video sharing (e.g., www.youtube.com). Cyberbullying disproportionately impacts LGBTQ students, with over half of LGBTQ students reporting having been cyberbullied within the past month (Kosciw, Greytak, Diaz, & Bartkiewicz, 2010). Methods of cyberbullying are varied and have unique features not present in in-person bullying, such as anonymity, impersonation (e.g., creating a false online identity and contacting a person), and masquerading (using another person's account when cyberbullying so that the actions will be traced back to that person instead of the actual bully) (Bauman, 2011; Trolley & Hanel, 2010). Alternately, some forms of cyberbullying closely resemble more traditional bullying, but use a digital format, including (Bauman, 2011; Trolley & Hanel, 2010):

- Denigration (providing defamatory information about someone);
- Publicizing information provided in confidence (a type of gossip or rumor spreading);
- Flaming (hostile messages or posts);
- Stalking (repeated harassment and threats);
- Exclusion (intentionally removing a person from an online group or encouraging others to exclude a person socially).

Currently, research on this relatively new phenomenon remains scarce, and scholars remain in debate regarding similarities and differences between in-person and cyberbullies, victims, and bystanders (Bauman, 2011). However, parallels between the two types of bullying suggest that the impact may be similar and that victims of cyberbullying are at risk for the same outcomes as in-person victims. In fact, several widely publicized youth suicides have been attributed to cyberbullying (De Nies, James, & Netter, 2010).

Cyberbullying has yet to be included in many states' antibullying legislation. Legal precedent (e.g., *Tinker v. Des Moines Independent Community School District*) suggests that schools can respond to off-campus speech (cyber or in person) that disrupts the educational process or interferes with a student's feelings of safety while on a school campus (Willard, 2007).

Due to the increasing rates of cyberbullying, school bully prevention teams should address this in both policy and practice. Some possibilities for this include (Bauman, 2011; Trolley & Hanel, 2010; Willard, 2007):

- Determine the prevalence of cyberbulling among students (and specifically for LGBTQ students);
- Create specific policy forms that outline acceptable uses for technology that require student and parent/guardian signatures (sometimes called Acceptable Use Policies);
- Include cyberbullying explicitly in anti-bullying and anti-harassment policies;
- Advertise and review policies frequently with students and parents;
- Educate students and parents about types of cyberbullying, potential impacts of cyberbullying, strategies for online safety, and appropriate responses to cyberbullying (e.g., take screenshots, download and print the evidence, alert school officials).

Programs Specifically Designed to Enhance the Safety of LGBTQ Students

Along with general bullying-prevention programming in schools, there are specific programs and strategies designed to specifically support LGBTQ students and help create safe, supportive climates for them. These are not designed to prevent or reduce acts of bullying or discrimination per se, however, they are designed to provide recognition, voice, and value to LGBTQ students and the LGBTQ community in general. These programs and activities are designed to empower LGBTQ students, taking some of the power back from those who have victimized and silenced them in the schools.

Gay-Straight Alliances (GSAs)

GSAs are non-curricular student organizations that strive to create safe and supportive environments for LGBTQ students and allies. Although it is difficult to estimate the current number of GSAs nationwide, the Gay-Straight Alliance Network (www.gsanetwork.org) reports that 50% of public high schools in California had GSAs in 2010. In contrast, there were only 32 GSAs in schools in Utah (Eckholm, 2011).

GSAs can benefit LGBTQ students in the following ways:

- Providing a strong social network and direct support (Hansen, 2007);
- Promoting advocacy skills (Mayberry, 2006);
- Practicing strategies for responding to harassment and bullying (Cooper-Nicols & Bowleg, 2010);
- Developing a more positive view of their own futures (Cooper-Nicols & Bowleg, 2010).

In fact, research has found that the impact of a GSA on positive school climate for LGBTQ youth is substantial. For example, in an evaluation of the multifaceted Massachusetts Safe Schools program (which included policy development, staff training, LGBTQ inclusive curriculum, and GSAs), GSAs were found to be the most salient factor in predicting a positive school climate (Szalacha, 2003).

GSA leaders provide another level of support for LGBTQ students, functioning as role models, liaisons, and sources of information (Graybill et al., 2009). Any staff member can advise a student group, and GSA advisors are often teachers, counselors, or psychologists. Although GSA advisors can potentially be an enormous asset to schools working to improve services for LGBTQ students, they also face certain risks. In a study involving GSA advisors, Valenti and Campbell (2009) found that both heterosexual and LGBT advisors encountered homophobia, both being accused of "recruiting" students into the LGBTQ community and feeling that their jobs were threatened. Concerns such as these highlight the importance of school policies that protect LGBT and ally staff from employment discrimination, as discussed in Chapter 4.

Given the widespread benefits of GSAs, the formation of one can be a critical step in promoting positive school climate. Fortunately, many quality resources exist to guide GSA formation, such as GLSEN (www.glsen.org), Lambda Legal (www.lamdalegal.org), American Civil Liberties Union (www.aclu.org), and GSA Network (www.gsanetwork.org). Many of the steps listed across these websites are similar, with suggestions including:

- Follow the guidelines established at your school for forming any non-curricular club;
- Identify an advisor;
- Inform school administration and guidance staff about the planned club;

- Keep records of all forms submitted for approval;
- Select a location;
- Advertise meetings.

In addition, these organizations provide information packets for students and staff with suggested activities and ideas for GSA participants, information on legal issues (as discussed in Chapter 4), and strategies for managing resistance from administration, parents, and school boards. A list of tips for students creating GSAs is included on the CD. Also included on the CD is a letter written by the American Civil Liberties Union (ACLU) to school administrators regarding the legal reasons why schools must allow students to form GSAs (contained in materials for Chapter 4).

Safe Space

Safe Space is a project created by GLSEN that identifies allies of LGBTQ students (and LGBT parents and their children) within the school community by placing small stickers outside of their doors, windows, or desk areas that identify them as a "Safe Space." This concept is in line with research that identifies the presence of supportive adults on campus as a protective factor for LGBTQ students (e.g., Cooper-Nicols & Bowleg, 2010; Murdock & Bolch, 2005; Orban, 2003). School staff with these stickers agree to be safe individuals for LGBTQ students to speak with, to ask for help or resources, to discuss concerns over safety, or to report incidents of bullying or harassment. The Safe Space kit is a low-cost resource available through GLSEN (www.safespace.glsen.org), and includes a sticker, posters that describe the program to the school community, and a resource guide for allies that provides suggestions for assisting and advocating for LGBTQ students.

GLSEN created a similar program targeting school-based athletics, called Safe Sports Space (http://sports.glsen.org/resources/safe-sports-space-campaign/) focusing on athletes, coaches, fans, and physical education students and teachers. Special posters and stickers have been designed for placement in gyms, locker rooms, trainers' and coaches' offices, playing fields, or other locations where sports are practiced and played, and resources are available for coaches, students, and administrators.

Remembrance Activities

LGBTQ advocacy organizations have designated specific days to recognize and commemorate LGBTQ issues. In schools that are including representation of LGBTQ issues throughout the curriculum and focusing on responsive climates, the recognition of these days can provide additional publicity to ongoing efforts to support LGBTQ students. One example is the Day of Silence (www.glsen.org), observed in April, which involves students spending a day in silence as a gesture to represent the impact (i.e., silencing) of bullying and harassment on LGBTQ students. A letter from the ACLU addressed to school administrators regarding the rights of students to participate in this event is included on the CD. Another example is the Transgender Day of Remembrance, celebrated on November 20, which memorializes the transgender individuals who have been killed due to their gender identity or gender expression (http://www.hrc.org/issues/transgender_day_of_remembrance.asp). As discussed in Chapter 6, it is important that these days and activities are not the only times of the year that schools recognize LGBTQ persons or issues. However, when they are held in conjunction with other efforts to create safe and supportive climates for LGBTQ students, such as inclusive curriculum and staff trainings, they can be powerful tools.

No Name Calling Week

No Name Calling Week is a national program developed by GLSEN that aims to draw attention to the problem of bullying on school campuses and to provide educators with a comprehensive set of lessons, activities, and resources addressing this topic in K–12 schools. Books, videos, training materials, lesson plans by grade level, and activities are available online (www.nonamecallingweek.org). Similar to the remembrance activities previously discussed, No Name Calling Week should not be implemented as the only step toward improving a school climate for LGBTQ students, but it can be a useful addition to other efforts.

Safe School Climates

The elimination of bullying and harassment of LGBTQ students requires a multifaceted approach. Bullying prevention and intervention programs should be implemented alongside actions such as the adoption of inclusive anti-bullying policies, the inclusion of LGBTQ information in school curricula, and school-wide trainings on diversity and LGBTQ issues. Each of these actions aims to impact the school climate, creating an environment where bullying and harassment of LGBTQ students is less likely to occur. Developing safe school climates requires a commitment to a vision of schools as places where all students can reach their potential and meaningfully contribute to larger society. There is a checklist for educators related to safe school climates on the accompanying CD.

Eight

Counseling
LGBTQ Students

Previous chapters of this book have highlighted the increased risk for social and emotional problems for LGBTQ students. As a result of bullying, discrimination, rejection, confusion, and all the mental health problems associated with these (e.g., depression, anxiety, school failure), LGBTQ students may seek or be referred for counseling at school. Additionally, like non-sexual minority students, LGBTQ students may experience other stressors or mental health issues typical of any adolescent. One of the primary tasks of the school-based mental health professional working with LGBTQ students is to determine what role, if any, sexual orientation or gender identity has in students' presenting problems (Dworkin, 2000; C. Ryan, 2001).

LGBTQ students may be in counseling because of issues directly related to their sexual orientation or gender identity. For example, students may be experiencing depression or anxiety as they begin to self-identify as LGBTQ. Similarly, students may seek or be referred to counseling because of issues that are related to or exacerbated by their sexual orientation or gender identity, such as relationship problems. Finally, students may be in counseling for issues completely unrelated to their sexual orientation or gender identity, such as learning self-management strategies for Attention Deficit/Hyperactivity Disorder or decreasing conflicts with teachers. Mental health professionals have a fine line to walk between ensuring that LGBTQ students know that they are free to talk about their identity and related issues in counseling and not assuming that this is the main cause of students' problems. This chapter explores issues in working with LGBTQ students in counseling when the presenting problems are directly or indirectly related to students' sexual orientation or gender identity.

Ethical Issues in Counseling LGBTQ Students

Major professional organizations, such as the American Psychological Association (APA), the National Association of School Psychologists (NASP), the American Counseling Association (ACA), the American School Counseling Association (ASCA), and the National Association of Social Workers (NASW) provide ethical guidelines for mental health professionals. The ethical mandates for working with LGBTQ students and families are similar across disciplines, highlighting the necessity for professionals to be aware of their own beliefs and biases related to sexual orientation and gender identity, to educate themselves about critical issues LGBTQ individuals face (e.g., discrimination, internalized homophobia), to respect individuals' rights and dignity, to advocate for equitable treatment, and to provide developmentally appropriate and affirmative counseling.

Most major professional organizations have developed position statements related to conversion or reparative therapy, which refers to counseling practices to change someone's sexual orientation. Such practices are considered unethical and do not have evidence to support their use. In alignment with major professional organizations, this chapter advocates counseling that supports, accepts, and validates LGBTQ sexual orientation and gender identity. If a mental health professional is unable to provide ethical treatment for an LGBTQ student, he or she is obligated to provide a referral to a counselor who can. More information about ethical standards can be found in "Just the Facts about Sexual Orientation and Youth: A Primer for Principals, Educators, and School Personnel" (Just the Facts Coalition, 2008), which is available on the accompanying CD in the resources for Chapter 2.

Preconditions of Counseling

Mental health professionals working with LGBTQ students need to have some basic knowledge about identity development and issues affecting LGBTQ individuals. Garnets, Hancock, Cochran, Goodchilds, and Peplau (1991) offer professionals some key preconditions that support counseling of LGBTQ students. First and foremost, professionals must believe and implicitly communicate to students that homosexuality and bisexuality are not forms of pathology and that sexual minority individuals can and do lead happy and fulfilling lives. Second, professionals should be aware that prejudice and discrimination can be overt or covert and can cause problems for LGBTQ students. Lastly, professionals recognize that sexual orientation or gender identity is only one aspect of the student and may not cause the student's problems.

Mental health professionals do not need to identify as LGBTQ themselves to be effective counselors for LGBTQ students (Garnets et al., 1991; Liddle, 1996), but they should employ good basic counseling skills. Research suggests that sexual minority individuals find counseling more helpful when they have a counselor who listens to and affirms them, displays understanding and empathy, normalizes their experiences, provides support and information, maintains a nonjudgmental stance, and ensures that unrelated problems are not misattributed to sexuality or gender identity (Israel, Gorcheva, Burnes, & Walther, 2008; Malley & Tasker, 2007).

When starting counseling, it is likely that mental health professionals will not know a student's sexual orientation or gender identity. Thus, it is important for professionals to use LGBTQ affirmative language with all students (Reynolds & Hanjorgiris, 2000). This not only includes using gender neutral language (e.g., saying "romantic interest" instead of boyfriend or girlfriend), but also involves having an openness to talking about issues of sexuality and gender (e.g., in an early session, the professional might offer a general statement such as, "Students come to talk to me about all kinds of things, like feeling sad, problems with friends and family, questions about sexual orientation, and difficulties in school"). Professionals are also encouraged to display diversity stickers or posters in their offices that address sexual orientation and gender identity, as this might make students feel more comfortable talking about themselves (Israel et al., 2008; Pope, Bunch, Szymanski, & Rankins, 2004). A variety of posters mental health professionals can display are included on the CD.

Supporting Identity Development and Coming Out

As discussed in more detail in Chapter 2, sexual minority identity development, self-labeling, and disclosure of sexual identity are ongoing processes for LGBTQ adolescents. Research suggests that these processes can create a great deal of anxiety for students, and are often associated with loneliness, isolation, and feelings of insecurity and vulnerability (Cowie & Rivers, 2000). Given this, mental health professionals have an important role to play in students' identity development and coming out processes. First and foremost, professionals must demonstrate a positive response to any revelation about sexual identity. This not only helps students feel accepted, but also signals that they are welcome to continue to explore their identity in a safe, therapeutic environment.

Hunter (2007) suggests that mental health professionals' primary goal for students in early stages of sexual identity development should be to help them explore and discover the identity that they feel fits them best. Professionals should validate students without putting pressure on them to choose a sexual identity. Students should feel free to express confusion and change their minds as many times as they need to as they grapple with better understanding their own sexual identity. As students begin to become more secure about their LGBTQ identity, they may benefit from exposure to and connection with affirming community organizations, either locally or online. This can help normalize students' experiences and provide them with role models. As students access these resources, their thoughts, ideas, and impressions about what they are learning and experiencing might help mental health professionals to better grasp how students are managing issues like internalized homophobia, attractions, and dating.

As students begin the disclosure process with others, mental health professionals can help students explore the benefits and drawbacks of disclosing their sexual identities or keeping them secret (Hunter, 2007). In reviewing the research on disclosure, Savin-Williams (1990, 1996) identified some benefits of disclosure, including:

- A decrease in feelings of loneliness and guilt;
- Greater feelings of freedom, acceptance, and genuineness.

Savin-Williams (1990, 1996) also identified some drawbacks of disclosure, including:

- Rejection and alienation from social support groups (e.g., peer group, family, cultural community);
- Violence and abuse;
- Expulsion from home.

Ultimately, coming out is a very personal decision for each student to make given his or her personal and social situation. The mental health professional's role in identity development is to help students explore how their sexual identity affects and interacts with other aspects of their identity and lives (Reynolds & Hanjorgiris, 2000).

Hunter (2007) suggests some ways in which mental health professionals can support students who are thinking about disclosure. Disclosure should be something that is done when it is in a student's best interest, and professionals might need to ask pointed questions about possible positive and negative consequences of disclosure to ensure that students have a realistic picture of what might occur. Second, professionals can engage students in discussions about the logistics of disclosure, identifying who they will tell and when and where they want to have the conversation. Related to this, professionals can help students practice how they will disclose their identity in a direct and positive manner that does not waiver (unless students are disclosing a questioning identity). By making more direct and positive statements ("I'm a lesbian and I'm happy" instead of "I think I might be a lesbian"), students leave less room for others to think they can talk the students out of it.

Hunter (2007) also suggests that it is critical for professionals to help students think about the worst thing that might happen when they disclose and how they might handle it. Similarly, if students are disclosing to family and think that they might be rejected, in physical danger, or kicked out of the house, a crisis plan needs to be in place. This plan should include phone numbers for hotlines and services, possible sources of emotional and financial support, and alternative living situations (e.g., shelters, friends, other family members). If this level of negative outcome is anticipated, mental health professionals should ensure that students are prepared for such a response and should help them explore the possibility of waiting to disclose until they are in a better position.

Homophobia

An issue that negatively affects students as they self-label and disclose their sexuality or gender identity is homophobia (or biphobia or transphobia), both internalized and societal (Dworkin, 2000; Reynolds & Hanjorgiris, 2000). Internalized homophobia/biphobia/transphobia is a broad-reaching phenomenon that occurs because individuals have been exposed to negative stereotypes and messages about LGBTQ groups from early childhood on (i.e., societal homophobia), and they have accepted and internalized these negative views (Dworkin, 2000). Reynolds and Hanjorgiris (2000) suggest that it is important for mental health professionals to address these issues in counseling, helping students to counteract internalized messages. This might be done by helping students understand how social and political forces have perpetuated these messages and using techniques to help students challenge and reframe these messages (Russell & Bohan, 2007). Cognitive-behavioral techniques may be particularly helpful in addressing homophobia/biphobia/transphobia (Fassinger, 2000).

A resource for professionals working with sexual minority individuals is *The Therapist's Notebook for Lesbian, Gay, and Bisexual Clients: Homework, Handouts, and Activities for Use in Psychotherapy* (Whitman & Boyd, 2003), which has a number of activities designed to address heterosexism and homophobia/biphobia. Although this book is designed primarily for use with adults, some activities can be easily modified for use with adolescents.

Suicide

Research on suicide rates for LGBTQ students as compared to their heterosexual peers is inconclusive, likely due to factors such as lack of information about sexual identity of youth who commit suicide and inaccurate rates of reporting suicide (Lieberman, Poland, & Cassel, 2008; Miller & Eckert, 2009). Regardless, suicide rates continue to be a concern for students across the board (Miller & Eckert, 2009), and many factors that put students at greater risk for suicide are more likely to be present for LGBTQ students as a result of their experiences as sexual minority individuals. These factors include depression, anxiety, substance abuse, peer victimization, social isolation, and family problems (Miller & Eckert, 2009). Thus, it is critical for mental health professionals working with LGBTQ students to assess and address suicide in counseling.

In counseling, it is recommended that professionals provide a forum for open discussion and ask pointed questions about suicide prior to it being raised by students, as evidence suggests that this can lead to positive outcomes for students (and it is considered a myth that talking about suicide might put the idea into someone's head) (Miller & Eckert, 2009). Lieberman et al. (2008) suggest that mental health professionals take any threat of suicide seriously, even if it is said jokingly or is contained in a school assignment. If it is determined that students are actively considering suicide, professionals should employ intervention techniques, such as assessing risk, ensuring constant supervision, talking with family members, and alerting appropriate agencies (Lieberman et al., 2008).

Even if students are not actively suicidal, professionals might consider providing LGBTQ students a list of resources that includes hotlines such as the National Suicide Prevention Lifeline (http://www.suicidepreventionlifeline.org; 1-800-273-TALK) and the GLBT National Help Center (http://www.glnh. org/index2.html; 1-888-843-4564).

Group Counseling

Although little has been written about group counseling for LGBTQ individuals in general, even less literature addresses group counseling for LGBTQ students. Group counseling with this population offers the potential for participants to have a safe space in which to openly explore their experiences and feel validated by others who likely share some common ground (DeBord & Perez, 2000; Miller, House, & Tyler, 2002). This may be particularly beneficial for LGBTQ students who often feel isolated in the larger school community. Group counseling for LGBTQ students should address similar concerns as individual counseling, such as identity development and disclosure, homophobia/biphobia/transphobia, suicide and other self-harm behaviors (e.g., substance use), relationships with friends and family, and school issues (Miller et al., 2002). Muller and Hartman (1998) offer an outline of a counseling group for sexual minority youth that includes sessions on family relationships, coming out, and homophobia, along with sessions to connect students with community resources and adult role-models. This may serve as a starting point for mental health professionals who are putting a group together. As with all interventions, it is recommended that outcome measures be utilized to begin the process of developing effective group curriculums (Fisher et al., 2008). Additionally, as will be discussed in more detail in the next section of this chapter, group leaders should take into account the unique experiences and needs of bisexual, questioning, and transgender students when considering group composition and developing group curriculum (Fisher et al., 2008).

Special Populations

Bisexual Students

Students who identify as bisexual may experience even greater marginality than students who identify as lesbian or gay, as they may not feel connected to or be accepted by the heterosexual or lesbian/gay community (Dworkin, 2000; Kennedy & Fisher, 2010; Matteson, 1996). The myth that bisexuality serves as a temporary identity on the way to identifying as lesbian or gay remains pervasive (Matteson, 1996). However, research suggests that over 60% of individuals who first identify as bisexual maintain this identity over time (Rosario, Scrimshaw, Hunter, & Braun, 2006), pointing to the relative stability of a bisexual identity (Kennedy & Fisher, 2010). It has been suggested that in counseling, it is helpful to acknowledge that individuals can indeed be attracted to both girls and boys (or women and men) and to give students permission to feel what they feel (Matteson, 1996). Additionally, mental health professionals in schools must be aware of biphobia, as a similar but separate phenomenon from homophobia, and its impact on bisexual students (Kennedy & Fisher, 2010). Biphobia is associated with a lack of knowledge about or visibility of bisexuality, and counselors can help bisexual students find appropriate resources (in communities or online) to provide them with information about and models of bisexuality (Kennedy & Fisher, 2010).

Questioning Students

Little has been written to distinguish questioning students from those who identify as lesbian, gay, or bisexual. However, in their 2008 study, Espelage, Aragon, Birkett, and Koenig identified some ways in which questioning students' experiences differed from their LGB and heterosexual peers. Specifically, they found that questioning students reported greater teasing and victimization, increased feelings of depression and suicidal ideation, and greater use of alcohol and marijuana than their LGB and heterosexual peers. Questioning students may be particularly vulnerable as they do not feel that they fit in with either the LGB or heterosexual social groups at school. Given this, mental health professionals need to be particularly aware of the impact that questioning one's sexual identity can have on students' well-being and school experiences. Counseling services for questioning students should validate students' experiences, allow questioning students to talk openly about their sexual identity, and provide support for exploration.

Transgender Students

As discussed in Chapter 2, transgender students most often receive a clinical diagnosis of Gender Identity Disorder (GID). Therapeutic treatment of GID is complex. Ethically, mental health professionals must grapple with considerations of whether or not GID is really a disorder rather than a variation of normal gender identity that is currently considered socially unacceptable (Zucker, 2006). This might be likened to the time when homosexuality was considered a disorder rather than a variation of sexual identity (until 1975 according to the American Psychological Association). As LGB sexual identity has gained greater social acceptance, it is no longer considered pathological in the views of most major professional psychological organizations. Will gender identity variations still be considered problematic if society becomes more accepting of broader views of gender? Even without a clear answer to this question, mental health professionals should let ethical guidelines (e.g., beneficence and nonmaleficence, respects for rights and dignity) shape their treatment approaches for transgender students.

Although often included in literature about LGBQ students, transgender students' experiences and needs differ from those of their sexual minority peers as they are managing gender identity issues along with possible sexual orientation issues. In their recent study of the experiences of adolescent transgender students, Greytak, Kosciw, and Diaz (2009) found that transgender students reported greater victimization and poorer educational outcomes than their LGB and heterosexual peers. Specifically, almost all transgender students reported being verbally harassed, more than half reported being physically harassed, and more than a quarter reported being physically assaulted because of their sexual orientation/gender identity. As discussed in Chapter 3, higher levels of harassment are associated with more negative school outcomes, such as skipping class and days of school, lower grade point averages, and fewer post-secondary school aspirations.

In clinical practice, research suggests that younger children with GID may be more responsive to therapeutic intervention, as their gender identity is more malleable by nature of their age (consider brain plasticity in young children) (Zucker, 2006). Therapeutic interventions with adolescents and young adults with GID have been much less successful in altering gender identification (Zucker, 2006). Instead, when gender identity seems to be the presenting problem, therapeutic interventions can focus on gender identity development and lifestyle changes.

Similar to the identity development of LGB students, transgender students' identity develops over time. Lennon and Mistler (2010) provide guidance for professionals in working with transgender adolescents during different stages of identity development. As a basic consideration, they encourage professionals to "respect and honor a transgender client's choices, including declared vocabulary and language (e.g., correct name and pronouns)" (p. 234). As transgender students are first becoming aware of their identity, it is suggested that counselors normalize students' experiences and help connect them to appropriate resources. Lennon and Mistler (2010) also note that there is a great deal of misinformation online that can be harmful for students, and professionals can help guide students to reputable resources. During these beginning stages of identity development, they also suggest that professionals focus on students' current experiences, including what it is like to talk about these issues with the counselor (e.g., fears of judgment from the counselor). As transgender students become ready to disclose their identity to others, professionals should engage in a similar process to what was described previously for disclosure for sexual minority students (e.g., evaluating costs and benefits, developing a disclosure script, having safety plans).

Lennon and Mistler (2010) also suggest some activities that will assist transgender students in identity development, such as:

- Keeping journals about their experiences and the meaning of identity and labels;
- Drawing pictures of themselves in 5 and 10 years to get a better sense of their perceived future and how they might want to live their lives;
- Making two collages, the first with pictures/words of things that describe them and the second with pictures/words of things that do not describe them.

Lennon and Mistler (2010) suggest that as transgender students move into later stages of identity development, issues around transitioning to live as their identified gender are likely to be the focus of counseling. Adolescents may seek sex reassignment through surgery and/or hormone treatment to align their external sex characteristics with their gender identity, but Zucker (2006) recommends that there are intermediary steps that mental health professionals can take in their work with adolescents. Professionals can help adolescents explore lifestyle changes that they can make to live more as their identified gender, as well as help them understand their sexual orientation (Zucker, 2006). Some transgender individuals might identify as heterosexual (e.g., an adolescent with the sex characteristics of a boy whose gender identity is that of a girl and who is attracted to boys most often identifies as heterosexual), and others may identify as lesbian, gay, bisexual, or questioning (or some other label). If students are seeking sex reassignment, the specifics of this might be considered outside the scope of school-based counseling services. However, it is important for professionals to educate themselves about the issues associated with sex reassignment and to connect students with medical and mental health professionals who are more experienced with these issues, in addition to providing school-based supports as needed.

Intersex Students

As discussed in Chapter 2, intersex students often experience a culture of silence around their condition (MacKenzie, Huntington, & Gilmour, 2009), which can lead to feelings of differentness, shame, and isolation (Lev, 2006). Lev (2006) provides guidelines for the treatment of intersex children/adolescents. First, intersex students should be provided with accurate information about their bodies and medical histories (as is age appropriate). Second, when children become mature enough, they should be included in decisions about their bodies and development, including surgeries and hormone therapy. Third, intersex students and their parents need to advocate so medical professionals ensure that students' bodies are treated in a respectful way during medical examinations to decrease feelings of alienation from and objectification of their bodies (e.g., not bringing a parade of residents through during the examination). Fourth, the support team, including students' parents, counselors, doctors, etc., need to allow students to determine the sex/gender with which they identify and make decisions accordingly. Finally, intersex students may need a private space, such as counseling, to explore issues of sex, sexuality, gender, etc., as not everything may be appropriate for discussion with parents and medical doctors.

Diversity Among LGBTQ Students

Research suggests that sexual minority identity development generally occurs around the same time for African American, Latino, and Caucasian youth, although differences exist in their participation in sexual minority-related social activities and level of disclosure (Parks, Hughes, & Matthews, 2004; Rosario, Scrimshaw, & Hunter, 2004). When counseling LGBTQ students, other aspects of their identities should be considered, as these characteristics help put sexuality or gender identity into a larger context of the whole person. Dworkin (2000), Lennon and Miller (2010), and Smith (1997) suggest that mental health professionals consider the importance students place on family, community, and religion (and the views of each regarding sexuality and gender identity), students' levels of acculturation and assimilation, and the intersection of race, ethnicity, religion, sexuality/gender identity, and history of oppression. Trying to balance these multiple aspects of identity can lead to greater identity conflict for LGBTQ students, as they may feel they are forced to choose between the LGBTQ community and their racial/ethnic community (and may feel that they cannot express all aspects of their identity in either community) (Pope, Mobley, & Myers, 2010).

Mental health professionals should recognize that there may be times that it is beneficial for LGBTQ students to suppress their sexual/gender identity to maintain close connections within their family, church, and/or racial/ethnic community (Pope et al., 2010; Smith 1997). These factors should be taken into account during discussion of self-labeling and disclosure, as coming out may have different costs for different students (Smith, 1997). If a student has explored the risks of disclosure and has made a decision to postpone disclosure, professionals can help that student identify the conditions under which he or she would feel more comfortable disclosing his or her sexual/gender identity.

Putting All the Pieces Together

School-based mental health professionals have the opportunity to support LGBTQ students during a potentially stressful time of life. By becoming more knowledgeable about LGBTQ identity development, by recognizing the phenomena of oppression, discrimination, and homophobia/biphobia/transphobia, and by viewing students as whole people comprised of many characteristics (with sexuality and gender identity being one part), professionals can better support students whose presenting problems are directly and indirectly related to their sexual orientation or gender identity. Listening, validating, and normalizing experiences are critical, along with helping students navigate the disclosure process and ensuring that students stay safe from others and themselves. Most of all, professionals can instill a sense of hope that students will successfully navigate the challenges of adolescence, and will feel happy and confident in themselves.

Case Studies

Javier

Mrs. Santos agrees that she will talk with Javier, if he consents to see her, but that she cannot ethically talk to Javier about "not being gay." She also informs his mother that if she talks with Javier, she will not reveal anything that he tells her as that would be breaking Javier's confidentiality. Javier's mother indicates that she understands. Later that day, Mrs. Santos calls Javier to her office. She tells him that his mother asked Mrs. Santos to talk to him, but that it is his decision as to whether or not he wants to talk with her. She also tells him about confidentiality and the limits of confidentiality. Javier asks questions about confidentiality, seeking assurances that what he talks about will not be shared with anyone in his family or with teachers at school. With this understanding, he tells Mrs. Santos that he needs someone to talk to because he is feeling confused about his life.

Over the next eight weeks, Mrs. Santos meets with Javier for individual counseling. Javier is quite forthcoming in the sessions, but often has difficulty putting his thoughts and feelings into words. Additionally, at times, he seems embarrassed or ashamed to admit his feelings to Mrs. Santos.

Mrs. Santos responds by actively listening and encouraging Javier to take the time he needs to express himself. She makes a concerted effort to phrase her questions and comments in ways that will communicate a nonjudgmental stance. She reflects his feelings and asks clarifying questions. During sessions, Javier talks a lot about how his family and friends view homosexuality as something wrong and sinful. He thinks they will reject him if they know. He expresses conflicting viewpoints, sometimes stating, "I think there must be something really wrong with me," and other times expressing things like, "This is just the way I am and I wish that people would just let me be me." Mrs. Santos encourages Javier to consider who he wants to be in the present and in the future, and she helps Javier explore what options might be possible for him (e.g., "What would it be like if you had to suppress this part of yourself?" "Can you envision a time when you might be able to tell people about your sexuality?").

Throughout the sessions, Mrs. Santos notices that Javier appears to be becoming more comfortable with his sexuality. During the eighth session, he comments, "You know, I'm glad that my mom knows. I wish she wouldn't be so upset about it, but at least one person in my life knows." Mrs. Santos asks Javier about how his relationship with his mom has been since she found out, and he replies that "She has been very watchful but also kind of protective." He explains that she has gotten on his father and older brother for giving him a hard time about girls, saying, "Don't pressure him. He'll get there when he's ready and he has college to focus on right now." After a moment of silence, during which Javier seems to be thinking about his mom, Mrs. Santos asks, "Javier, what would you think about talking more with your mom about your sexuality?" Javier expresses openness to the idea, and thinks that having Mrs. Santos there to support him will be helpful. Mrs. Santos agrees to call Javier's mom to invite her to attend a session with them next week.

Jessie

The school psychologist meets with Jessie's parents the week before school begins. She asks if Jessie has ever been in counseling, and Jessie's parents report that she has worked intermittently with a counselor for many years, as has the family to learn ways to support her gender identity and transition. The school psychologist and family discuss whether or not Jessie should receive school-based counseling. Ultimately, they decide that because Jessie's academics are strong and she is in a "good place" emotionally, that she will not require counseling at this time. They agree to revisit this should any issues arise, and that the school psychologist will meet Jessie during the first week of school to let her know that she can come to the school psychologist's office any time as a "Safe Space."

Nine

Supporting LGBTQ Parents and Their Children

Parents who are LGBTQ and their children have unique experiences when interacting with the school system. LGBTQ-parented families face risks and challenges in schools, such as having their families devalued in the classroom and managing myths and stereotypes about their families. Yet, with some small changes, teachers and other school staff can make schools more welcoming and responsive to these families.

Families with LGBTQ Parents

Estimates of the number of LGBTQ persons who are parents or guardians of school-aged children range from a few million up to around 15 million (e.g., Jeltova & Fish, 2005; Koerner & Hulsebosch, 1996). The exact numbers remain elusive because many LGBTQ adults do not elect to disclose their identities, either on general surveys (e.g., U.S. Census) or in school settings (Jeltova & Fish, 2005). What is known is that in any given school district, employees have knowingly or unknowingly worked with parents who are LGBTQ (Fox, 2007).

Several factors may explain why school staff may be unaware of the sexual identities and familial constellations that exist within the families of their students. One may be that parents are purposefully concealing their identities due to fear of discrimination and a desire to protect their children from harassment or mistreatment. Another explanation may be heteronormativity, or the general expectation that all individuals are heterosexual. From this perspective, educators are assuming that all parents are heterosexual and may fail to recognize that parents are LGBTQ unless these parents specifically identify themselves. Additionally, school staff may hold misconceptions about LGBTQ individuals, such that they only associate stereotypical imagery, dress, and behaviors with LGBTQ identities, thus failing to recognize the true identities of parents that do not fit their stereotype of an LGBTQ person (Jeltova & Fish, 2005).

The diversity within the group of individuals who may be labeled as LGBTQ parents is remarkable. Although these phrases may immediately conjure simple images such as families with two lesbian mothers and two gay fathers, the reality is that there is a virtually limitless range of family constellations in the United States. First, educators must understand that not all families have a foundation of biological relationships: adoptive and foster families are common among both sexual minority and heterosexual families. Also, it must be recognized that not all families consist of only one or two parental figures. If school staff want to understand and support all families, they must be aware that for some children, there are three or more individuals who fulfill parental roles. Finally, in order to embrace the diversity within this group, it must be recognized that parents can be lesbian, gay, or represent various iterations of the LGBTQ nuclear or extended family. For example, a child's family may consist of a biological father, a lesbian biological mother and her partner, or perhaps an adoptive lesbian mother and her transgender partner. When thinking about LGBTQ-headed families, it is important that school professionals remain open to and aware of the various family structures that are possible (this is true for LGBTQ and heterosexual families). A way to maintain this awareness is to define a family as consisting of people who love and support the child, and who fulfill parental roles and duties. By broadening definitions of family, school professionals will be more able to provide personalized supports for all students and caregivers.

Myths and Obstacles Faced by LGBTQ Parents

One of the largest obstacles for parents that are LGBTQ in the school system is that they are largely ignored and overlooked. Diverse family constellations are rarely discussed or represented in educational contexts, leaving children from such families at risk of receiving the message that their families are abnormal, inferior, or shameful (Kozik-Rosabal, 2000). The presumption of heterosexuality regarding parents and families may lead to decisions about curriculum and school-based social events (such as a Mother's Day activity, a heredity project based on a child's biological family, or a Father-Daughter luncheon) that may indirectly harm students from LGBTQ-parented families (Kozik-Rosabal, 2000), or create a culture where parents who are LGBTQ are devalued (Koerner & Hulsebosch, 1996). Additionally, many school staff may not be aware of how to approach a variety of situations involving parents who are LGBTQ or have the confidence to do so, such as (Ryan & Martin, 2000):

- Addressing LGBTQ individuals in general;
- Addressing parents and other important family members who are LGBTQ;
- Discussing LGBTQ relationships and family dynamics with parents;
- Representing LGBTQ-parented families in the curriculum;
- Responding to student questions about LGBTQ-parented families;
- Discussing family constellations including LGBTQ parents without addressing controversial issues such as gay marriage;
- Responding if students make negative comments about parents or other individuals who are LGBTQ.

Another obstacle for parents who are LGBTQ is the wide range of myths, misconceptions, and prejudices about LGBTQ parenting. In general, all LGBTQ persons are faced with societal questioning of the legitimacy of their so-called lifestyle. Myths about LGBTQ individuals include inflammatory beliefs such as associations with pedophilia, drug addiction, and emotional and physical illness (Kozik-Rosabal, 2000). LGBTQ people who are parents may face additional biases, particularly the myth that their children will grow up to be psychologically harmed or damaged, or that they will be LGBT (Jeltova & Fish, 2005). These harmful and inaccurate beliefs may lead many educators to assume that LGBTQ-headed families are inherently unhealthy or otherwise inferior to heterosexual-headed families (Ryan & Martin, 2000).

Contemporary psychological and sociological research has proven that these beliefs are false. For example, in a meta-analysis of over 20 studies regarding children from LGBT-headed families, Stacey and Biblarz (2001) concluded that LGBT parents are as effective as heterosexual parents, and that there were no differences in children from LGBT parents in factors such as depression, self-esteem, and anxiety. Nonetheless, these myths remain socially pervasive and are fueled by authors such as Paul Cameron, whose work espouses false information regarding LGBT parents "damaging" their children. Cameron's work has been heavily criticized by the academic community as being unethical and without scientific rigor, and he has been expelled from professional associations such as the American Psychological Association, the American Sociological Association, and the Canadian Psychological Association (http://psychology.ucdavis.edu/rainbow/html/facts_cameron_sheet.html). However, in spite of the misinformation propagated by a few individuals and organizations, experts remain hopeful that societal views, including social visibility and acceptance of LGBTQ parenting, have slowly improved in recent decades (Kozik-Rosabal, 2000; Ryan & Martin, 2000).

In addition to findings that children of parents who are LGBTQ score similarly on outcome measures of mental health and well-being, experts such as Stacey and Biblarz (2001) caution that researchers and educators should not ignore the differences that do exist. These authors suggest that the need to establish that children from parents who are LGBTQ are *equal*, or *not at greater risk than* children from heterosexual parents (in order to dispel myths and combat discrimination) may have led researchers to ignore critical differences that distinguish these youth as a unique population. Specifically, we know that children of LGBTQ parents are more likely to face harassment and discrimination at school than their classmates from non-sexual minority parented families (as discussed later in this chapter). Additionally, many LBGTQ individuals begin their families with adoption or foster parenting. These are differences that may exist regarding students with parents who are LGBTQ, and ignoring these differences may prevent school professionals from fully addressing the needs of these youth.

Experiences of LGBTQ Parents in K–12 Schools

There is a general lack of research about the experiences of parents who are LGBTQ in the educational system. To date, only one large-scale national study has been conducted. Completed as a joint project between the Gay, Lesbian, and Straight Education Network (GLSEN), the Family Equality Council, and Children of Lesbians and Gays Everywhere (COLAGE), this study examined surveys from 588 LGBT parents of K–12 students (Kosciw & Diaz, 2008). The results from this study illuminated the ways in which LGBT parents are similar and different from heterosexual parents. For example, compared to heterosexual parents, LGBT parents were more likely to be involved in (Kosciw & Diaz, 2008):

- Volunteering at school (46% of LGBT parents vs. 32% of national sample);
- Being members of the Parent-Teacher Association (PTA) (41% vs. 26%);
- Attending school events such as parent-teacher conferences (94% vs. 77%).

Similarly, parents who are LGBT reported being active communicators with their child's school, with about two-thirds of the sample reporting having spoken with school staff about being LGBT, and nearly one-half reporting having spoken with the school's principal within the past year.

Unfortunately, LGBT parents also reported a number of negative experiences involving schools. These experiences include (percentages are approximate) (Kosciw & Diaz, 2008):

- 27% reported experiencing hostile behavior from school staff, parents, or students (e.g., dirty looks, verbal hostility, derogatory remarks);
- 25% were mistreated by other parents in the school community;
- 15% heard negative comments about themselves or their families from other parents;
- 20% heard negative comments about themselves or their families from students at their child's school;
- 15% felt that their family was not acknowledged by their child's school;
- 5% reported that their parenting skills were questioned by a school staff member because of their LGBT identities.

Not unexpectedly, parents who felt excluded from their child's school were less likely to be actively involved there.

Finally, LGBT parents reported having worries or concerns about the safety of their children, with nearly 30% reporting being worried about student safety *some of the time* or more (Kosciw & Diaz, 2008). Similarly, about half of the parents who participated in this study reported worries that their children would have trouble making friends because they had LGBT parents (Kosciw & Diaz, 2008). Although research on this population is scarce, the findings from the Kosciw and Diaz (2008) study reflect similar points as those reported by other authors (e.g., Family Equality Council, 2008; Kozik-Rosabal, 2000) in that parents who are LGBTQ worry about their children being harassed or bullied in the school setting.

Experiences of Children of LGBTQ-Headed Families in Schools

As a part of the same study, Kosciw and Diaz (2008) also surveyed 154 students (ages 13–20) from LGBT-parented homes. Results from the students echo the findings from their parents in many ways. For example, the parents in this study reported concerns over their children's safety and treatment at school. Reports from their students demonstrate that these concerns are not unfounded; children who have parents who are LGBT face unique challenges with regard to safety, discrimination, and harassment. Specifically, due to stereotypes regarding perceived sexual orientation (i.e., youth are assumed to be LGBTQ if they have an LGBT parent), this group of youth may face discrimination based both upon their parents' LGBT status, as well as due to their own perceived sexual orientation. For example (percentages are approximate):

- 25% felt unsafe at school due to issues related to their families;
- 21% felt unsafe due to their actual or perceived sexual orientation;
- 45% experienced verbal harassment related to their families;
- 38% experienced verbal harassment related to their actual or perceived sexual orientation;
- 25% heard negative comments about their parents from other parents at school;
- 15% heard negative comments about their parents from teachers.

Additionally, students reported that their families were not recognized at their schools. A large portion of youth (over 33%) reported that school staff ignored their family, 22% of youth reported at least one teacher had discouraged them from talking about their family at school, and 20% had felt excluded from classroom activities because of their family.

These percentages show where schools and teachers have room to grow regarding the equal treatment of all students. Although this survey did not ask if students observed the teacher encouraging other students to speak about their heterosexual parents, it is reasonable to presume that teachers asked students not to talk about their family at school because they had parents who were LGBTQ. As discussed earlier in this chapter, perhaps the teachers feared that they would not know how to respond to student questions about this family. Regardless of the intention, teachers should be aware that even simple actions such as this can send students the message that their families are inferior in some way.

Results from this survey reflect findings from other authors and organizations working with youth from LGBTQ-parented families, who report similar risks of harassment and exclusion (e.g., COLAGE, Fenton, & Gilomen, 2005; Family Equality Council, 2008; Joltova & Fish, 2005). Other concerns that have been noted by researchers include a variety of out-of-school social situations. For example, children from LGBTQ-headed families might worry (based on experience or observation) that other parents might not let their kids come over to play at their house, that they will not be invited into other children's homes, or that teachers and other students might assume that they are LGBTQ (Family Equality Council, 2008).

Strategies to Create Welcoming Environments for LGBTQ-Headed Families

Chapters 5 and 6 of this book provide an overview of trainings and strategies that can make classrooms and other school environments inclusive of all students. Many of these strategies also serve the purpose of making schools welcoming for LGBTQ parents and students from LGBTQ-headed families (e.g., elementary curriculum that includes references to all kinds of family constellations).

School professionals, including teachers, administrators, school psychologists, and school counselors, generally agree parental involvement in education promotes academic success for students. In fact, some professional practice guidelines, such as those for the National Association of School Psychologists (NASP) identify the fostering of collaborative home-school relationships to be among the primary tasks for school-based practitioners (www.nasponline.org). However, if school professionals are committed to this concept, they must ensure that they create welcoming environments for all parents.

The first step is to create an environment that reflects the school's commitment to embracing all families. Visual signals of this include posters that represent parents that are LGBTQ and their children in a school's hallways or library, as well as age-appropriate books that include representations of diverse family constellations (Family Equality Council, 2008; Fox, 2007). Another way in which schools can portray this message is to specifically mention LGBTQ-parented families in school policies (Jeltova & Fish, 2005). Finally, schools can create welcoming environments by including LGBTQ-headed families in all tangible aspects of the school, such as newsletters, websites, and contact lists (Jeltova & Fish). For example, schools can include all members of the familial constellation on published family contact lists, or allow interested families to post familial celebrations (e.g., including adoptions, marriages, or partnerships) in school newsletters.

By creating a school environment that portrays nondiscriminatory and inclusive practices, parents that are LGBTQ may feel more acknowledged and welcomed to participate in their child's school. Many scholars believe that the ideal scenario is that all families are open regarding their family constellation, as this facilitates communication and collaboration between the school and the family, and allows the school to design any needed supports (Ryan & Martin, 2000). However, schools should never assume that they are aware of every LGBTQ-parented family in their community.

As discussed in Chapter 5, schools may face resistance when implementing efforts to make schools more welcoming regarding a variety of topics involving LGBTQ individuals. For example, an administrator who puts up a poster that includes a picture of parents who are LGBTQ with their children may fear being accused of pushing the "gay agenda" (Fox, 2007), or teachers may not want to address a book that includes a LGBTQ-parented family because they worry that a conversation about sex is not appropriate for their grade level. In these cases, educating school professionals about the importance of being inclusive to all types of families may help to address concerns and change practices. This education may include the fact that the only "agenda" being promoted is the one to ensure that all students and families are welcome and valued members of a school's community (Fox, 2007).

Using Appropriate Language

Using appropriate language and terminology is an important way to convey an inclusive message to parents who are LGBTQ. For example, the use of gender-neutral terms (e.g., partner vs. husband/wife) is recommended (Kozik-Rosabal, 2000). Additionally, educators should be careful to use language that does not imply the sexual identity of the entire family. Terms such as *gay family* or *LGBTQ family* may imply that the sexual orientation of students is related to that of their parents or guardians, thus perpetuating a dangerous stereotype. Instead of these terms, more specific terms such as "gay parents" or "two moms" are preferred (Fox, 2007). Similarly, references to "nontraditional families," or to a student's "real mom" or "natural mom" may imply deviance or inferiority and should not be used (Fox, 2007; Ryan & Martin, 2000). Teachers and other school staff should ask families for the terms that they prefer, as well as the names that their students may use for important adults in their lives (e.g., Daddy and Papa Mike) (Family Equality Council, 2008; Fox, 2007). When meeting any family for the first time, neutral language should be used. For example, if teachers are meeting a child's parent or guardian for the first time, they might ask "Who would you like us to include in discussions about your family?" (Family Equality Council, 2008).

When discussing family constellations in a school setting, educators should remember their obligations regarding confidentiality. As discussed in Chapter 4, both parents and students have a right to privacy, and disclosure of a parent or guardian's identity would be a serious violation of the rights of the family. It might be prudent to ask if a parent or guardian has shared his or her identity with other members of the community (e.g., "How open are you about your family with other members of the community?"; Family Equality Council, 2008), in order to ensure that privacy is not violated.

Developing Forms That Recognize LGBTQ-Headed Families

In addition to using inclusive, neutral language when communicating with all families within the school community, school professionals should update enrollment and other forms to ensure inclusiveness. For example, letters home should be addressed to families (e.g., Dear Family) rather than to a mother and a father (e.g., Dear Mom and Dad) (Fox, 2007).

Similarly, enrollment forms should utilize terms such as *Parent or Guardian*, and should allow space beneath these labels to allow all parents to complete forms in a way that best represents their families without needing to alter preprinted materials (Fox, 2007; Jeltova & Fish, 2005). For example, a parent completing the form might receive a mixed message when the form uses the inclusive term *parent* but provides two response lines, and therefore assumes that students all come from two-parent households.

Knowing the Law

Chapter 4 reviews the various laws and policies that impact LGBTQ students in schools. As discussed, the equal protection clause of the 14th Amendment, Title IX, as well as state and district anti-discrimination, anti-harassment, and anti-bullying laws and policies all protect students from discrimination, bullying, and harassment. Many of these same laws and policies similarly protect students of parents who are LGBTQ. For example, if a student is being harassed because she has a parent who is transgender, the school staff must investigate and respond to the harassment as they would any other case of harassment in order to provide equal protection. Similarly, if that student was harassed in a sexual nature, she would be protected by Title IX. State laws and school policies that specify prohibitions of discrimination, harassment, or bullying may be slightly different in their application to students from LGBTQ-parented homes. In these cases, students are often harassed due to their *perceived* sexual orientation. For this reason, it is important that policymakers include specific reference to perceived sexual orientation and perceived gender identity when they are enumerating protected groups.

An interesting application of law regarding LGBTQ parents and their children involves the recommended inclusion of diverse family constellations in school curriculum (discussed earlier in this chapter as well as in Chapter 6). Occasionally, these suggestions are considered controversial, and steps to prevent the inclusion of information regarding LGBTQ parents have been taken by districts and school boards. One example of this is Opt In/Opt Out policies that are sometimes utilized to allow parents to exclude their students from topics such as sex education, prevention of sexually-transmitted diseases, and human sexuality. These policies may be misapplied to allow parents to prevent their children from receiving information about diverse family structures in elementary school. This is not an appropriate application for these policies because discussions about different types of families do not need to include information about sex (www.welcomingschools.org).

Finally, when working with parents who are LGBTQ and their children, it is important for school professionals to become familiar with the laws regarding LGBTQ partnerships, marriages, and adoptions in their state. Although these laws do not impact who schools can contact, put on emergency lists, or invite to participate in educational meetings for a student, they are relevant to families and may help school professionals to better understand each family with whom they work.

Classrooms That Support Children with LGBTQ Parents

As discussed in Chapter 6, most curricula ignore LGBTQ identities and persons. Similarly, diverse family structures are rarely addressed in schools. As a result, students from LGBTQ-parented families may only see heterosexual parents represented and celebrated in schools, thus receiving the message that heterosexual families are superior or that their family is not healthy or legitimate (Kozik-Rosabal, 2000). Solutions to this include those discussed in Chapter 6, such as discussing LGBTQ parents in lessons and activities and including age-appropriate books that include LGBTQ persons and LGBTQ parents as characters. Additionally, teachers should be sensitive to classroom lessons and activities that presume heterosexual parents. For example, celebrations and classroom activities involving Mother's Day or Father's Day do not consider children of diverse family constellations (Family Equality Council, 2008; Fox, 2007). Similarly, lessons or activities that require students to study heredity traits in their family (e.g., eye color of biological relatives) presume that all children are living with biological parents, which is not the reality in today's classrooms (Fox, 2007). These type of lessons may be modified (e.g., allowing students to make as many Mother's Day cards as they like, suggesting that students prepare gifts for anyone who has been present in their lives in a parental role), or if deemed inappropriate, removed from classroom agendas.

Another suggestion for making sure that classrooms are welcoming for children from LGBTQ-parented homes is to consider diverse family constellations when providing materials for games or toys that involve families. For example, if a dollhouse includes only one male and one female adult doll to represent "parents," the toy is not representing all family types. Instead, it is recommended that additional male and female dolls are provided, as well as one or two older dolls that could represent grandparents or other care providers in order to help all children represent their families (Fox, 2007).

Training Programs

Many of the barriers to creating inclusive school communities for parents who are LGBTQ involve fears and misconceptions on the part of teachers, administrators, and other parents. Ryan and Martin (2000) describe several obstacles to supporting LGBTQ-parented families in schools, including: homophobic beliefs or prejudices of school staff, concern that coverage of any LGBTQ issues means focusing on sex, fears about being asked questions by students or heterosexual parents that they don't know how to answer, and discomfort with knowing how to appropriately address parents. As discussed in Chapter 5, staff education is an important way to address these concerns, and, therefore, a key component of the change process.

Staff training on the unique qualities of parents and families who belong to the LGBTQ community may include broad multicultural, diversity, and anti-bias training, as addressed in Chapter 5. However, it should also include topics specific to this population, including (Family Equality Council, 2008; Ryan & Martin, 2000):

- The needs and challenges faced by parents who are LGBTQ;
- Discussions of appropriate language;
- Suggestions for how teachers and staff can address parents who are LGBTQ;
- Learning how to reconcile personal beliefs with ethical and professional responsibilities;
- Inclusion of diverse families in classroom curricula;
- Creating administrative policies that are supportive of diverse families.

There are a few training materials available that help to meet these needs. As introduced in Chapter 5, The Human Rights Campaign (2009) created Welcoming Schools (lesson plans are available on the CD in the Chapter 5 section). Welcoming Schools is a comprehensive program that includes education components regarding diversity, types of families, and bullying. The website, www.welcomingschools.org, provides a rich array of resources, including handouts for parents and teachers, as well as lessons and activities for students, staff, and parents.

Another resource for staff training regarding LGBTQ-parented families are the numerous films on this topic, such as *In my Shoes, Both of my Moms' Names are Judy* and *It's Elementary* (Family Equality Council, 2008). Trainers could schedule a showing of these or similar films, and guide teachers, administrators, or parents in a discussion about parents who are LGBTQ, asking questions such as:

- "How are the families in the film similar to or different from your families?"
- "What were you surprised to learn from the families or students in this film?"
- "What could our school do to support a family like the one featured in the film?"

As research has shown that parents who are LGBTQ may face discrimination from other parents, it is especially important that training be provided to the broad school community, including parents, counselors, school board members, and other key figures. Additionally, educational training programs need to be proactive in providing information about families who have members in the LGBTQ community, as well as children from LGBTQ-parented homes. School psychologists, counselors, administrators, and teachers could be trained to work with this population at the start of the year, thus minimizing the need for reactive staff training (Jeltova & Fish, 2005).

Welcoming All Families

Students with parents who are LGBTQ may face similar discrimination, harassment, or bullying as students who are LGBTQ themselves. Often, these behaviors stem from myths and misinformation regarding LGBTQ parenting, such as LGBTQ parents automatically having LGBTQ children, or being inferior parents compared to heterosexual ones. With school-wide education for teachers, staff, students, and parents, all members of a school's community can learn that parents who are LGBTQ are just *parents*—they share the same concerns about their student's education and safety as all other parents. Additionally, this education can help create a school climate that not only tolerates, but *welcomes* all students and families. A handout on welcoming all families is available on the CD.

Case Study

Sydney

Throughout the process of Sydney's evaluation for special education, Mr. Green and the school psychologist developed a trusting working relationship. After the IEP meeting that established Speech/Language services for Sydney, Mr. Green asks to speak with the school psychologist about a concern. Mr. Green points out that the monthly school newsletter that he and Mr. Homer receive from the school is addressed to "The Mother and Father of Sydney Green." Mr. Green stated that although this is a small concern, it makes him feel as if the school does not respect his family. The school psychologist thanks Mr. Green for his willingness to share this concern, and asks him for his opinions regarding what the school can do to make sure that all families feel included. Mr. Green says that he will keep this request in mind and will let the school psychologist know if any other specific forms or letters catch his attention.

With Mr. Green's comments in mind, the school psychologist begins to review all of the school's paperwork and forms. He notices that in nearly all cases, forms are addressed "To the Mother and Father of ..." or to "Mr. and Mrs. _____." Although Mr. Green and Mr. Homer are the first LGBTQ parents that he has been aware of at this school, he reasons that there must have been others he was not aware of, and that there will be more in the future. He asks for a meeting with the principal to discuss modifying all documents and forms of communication used by the school to make them more inclusive of all families. His goal in making these modifications is to help parents like Mr. Green and Mr. Homer to form first impressions of the school that involve it being a safe place where their family is respected and understood.

Ten

Supporting Families of LGBTQ Students

Up to 75% of sexual minority adolescents who live at home have disclosed their identity to at least one parent (D'Augelli, Hershberger, & Pilkington, 1998). At some point in their teenage years, LGBTQ students will grapple with whether or not to tell, who to tell, and when to tell family members about their sexual orientation or gender identity. More LGBTQ youth are coming out to their families at earlier ages, in part due to increasing social and political visibility and acceptance of LGBTQ individuals (Martin, Hutson, Kazyak, & Scherrer, 2010). For professionals working with LGBTQ students in schools, having an awareness of the interplay between families and their LGBTQ children and having strategies to support families of LGBTQ students is important.

Background

Some LGBTQ students make a decision to disclose their identity to one or more family members, while others may have their identity discovered in some way (Hillier, 2002). In either case, there is an impact on the family system. Families' reactions right after disclosure and their long-term adjustment can help or hinder students' development.

When students choose to disclose their identity, they most often tell their mother or sister first (D'Augelli et al., 1998; Heatherington & Lavner, 2008; Hunter, 2007; Savin-Williams, 2003). It is difficult to predict how family members will react to LGBTQ students' disclosure of sexual/gender identity. However, research of the past 20 years suggests that reactions are generally negative, including feelings of shock, denial, anger, guilt, shame, and fear (Ben-Ari, 1995; Patterson, 2000; Saltzburg, 2004; Savin-Williams, 2003) that can escalate to physical violence and ejection from the home (Pilkington & D'Augelli, 1995; Savin-Williams, 2003). Many factors may influence parental reactions, including the parent's level of education about homosexuality (including misinformation), religious beliefs, and homophobia (Orban, 2003).

In her qualitative study of parents' reactions to disclosure, Saltzburg (2004) found that parents expressed a range of responses. Many parents reported an early awareness of their child's differentness, with some confiding in others about their observations and feelings long before their child's disclosure. However, this early awareness seemed to be followed by a period of denial, as parents reported feeling surprised by their child's ultimate disclosure. Another theme that emerged from Saltzburg's (2004) study was parents struggling to come to terms with their own internalized homophobia and managing the cognitive dissonance created by having a sexual minority child (i.e., internal feelings of tension caused by having negative feelings about homosexuality while having positive/loving feelings about their sexual minority child). During this time, parents reported feelings of isolation from their social support networks as they often did not share with others about their child's sexual orientation, reporting that they did not think others would understand their experiences. Similarly, parents reported feelings of estrangement from their child, focusing on the differences between their child and themselves and wondering what role they would play in their child's life as a sexual minority individual. Overall, parents appeared to manage their emotions better and to demonstrate greater adjustment when they gathered information, connected with other parents, and sought out experiences with other LGBTQ individuals.

Certainly, a number of LGBTQ youth who disclose their identities experience negative familial reactions, but this might be an incomplete picture (Diamond & Butterworth, 2008; Heatherington & Lavner, 2008). There have always been parents who embrace their child's identity from the beginning, easily accepting the new (or perhaps already suspected) aspect of their child. In addition, increased visibility and acceptance of LGBTQ individuals over the last few years in social, political, and media circles have changed the landscape for some LGBTQ youth and their families (Martin et al., 2010; Savin-Williams, 2003). Parents coming of age during this time are more accepting of sexual and gender diversity may react differently to their child's disclosure, and social and political forces may positively impact the family's adjustment after disclosure (Martin et al., 2010; Savin-Williams, 2003). Contemporary research suggests that family functioning after disclosure might be an indication of family functioning before disclosure (and vice versa), with families who demonstrate more cohesion, adaptability, flexibility, and social support faring better (Goodrich & Gilbride, 2010; Reeves et al., 2010). Additionally, research suggests that families go through a process of adjustment after the initial disclosure and, eventually, most families accept their child's identity (Goodrich & Gilbride, 2010).

Not surprisingly, greater family acceptance and a more positive family environment are associated with more positive adjustment for LGBTQ youth, such as higher self-esteem, greater social support, and better overall general health (Heatherington & Lavner, 2008; Padilla, Crisp, & Rew 2010; Ryan, Russell, Huebner, Diaz, & Sanchez, 2010). Conversely, lower family acceptance and rejection are associated with poorer outcomes, such as greater incidence of depression, substance abuse, and suicidal ideation and attempts (Rosario, Schrimshaw, & Hunter, 2009; Ryan et al., 2010). Thus, it is important for school professionals to have some tools to help families of LGBTQ students navigate both the initial disclosure and the longer-term process of accepting their LGBTQ child.

Family Diversity

In the increasingly multicultural landscape of families, it is important to consider the multiple identities families hold as these add complexity to the family system (Heatherington & Lavner, 2008). Although the research is sparse, there is evidence that sexual minority youth from diverse racial and ethnic backgrounds are less likely to disclose sexuality/gender identity to parents (Heatherington & Lavner, 2008). This may be due to issues of respecting cultural values, concerns about how those in the cultural community will view the family, and gender role expectations (Heatherington & Lavner, 2008).

Religion may play an important role in how families react to having an LGBTQ child. Religiosity is associated with more emphasis on traditional values, such as marriage and having children, which may in turn be related to more negative views of homosexuality (Heatherington & Lavner, 2008). LGBTQ individuals have been found to be less likely to disclose in more highly religious families (Heatherington & Lavner, 2008), and if they do disclose, more highly religious families are reported to be less accepting of their LGBTQ family members (Ryan et al., 2010).

While family diversity certainly adds complexity to the issue, within it there also exist opportunities to define and redefine what it means to be a family with an LGBTQ child. This includes a closer examination of cultures and subcultures in which the family exists and helping family members manage multiple aspects of their individual and familial identities. Families naturally grow, change, and adapt to new situations (e.g., birth, retirement, new homes, death), and most families make continual adjustments to maintain familial relationships. By understanding how families have responded to these types of experiences, professionals can draw on families' strengths to build support for the LGBTQ child.

Considerations for Family Counseling

The first consideration for family counseling is to ensure that students have disclosed their identity to their family. Mental health professionals should never put themselves in the position where they are "outing" students to their families. Professionals may provide a safe space for students to tell their families, role-play with students how to disclose to their families, and facilitate conversations between students and families, but ultimately, students should be the ones to disclosure their identity.

When providing counseling services for LGBTQ students and their families, mental health professionals may have to balance competing demands, the most significant being the possible competing needs of LGBTQ students and the needs of their families. This may require professionals to work with students and families separately to ensure that conjoint sessions will, at the very least, not cause emotional harm for students (Savin-Williams, 1996). As students become more confident in their identity, and families are able to express negative feelings in a productive manner, conjoint sessions are more appropriate (Savin-Williams, 1996). Similarly, if parents are generally comfortable with their child's identity from the beginning, conjoint sessions can help start ongoing conversations about the child's identity, disclosures to others, relationships, concerns, feelings, and expectations (Savin-Williams, 1996).

When working with LGBTQ students around family issues, it can be helpful for professionals to help students understand that it might take family members time to come to terms with students' LGBTQ identity. Savin-Williams (1996) suggests that mental health professionals help students recognize that it took them a period of time to accept and understand their own identity, and that they might need to be patient as their families go through a similar process after disclosure. Professionals can also help students develop or maintain more confidence in their sexuality or gender identity and to express this in a positive and unequivocal manner with family members (Hunter 2007).

At the core of family counseling, whether working with the family separately or with the student present, is to keep returning to the love that family members have for the child (Hunter, 2007). It might be helpful for each family counseling session to start and end with this in some manner, such as "You are here today because you love your daughter" or "Even with all these other feelings swirling around during this time, the love you feel for your son is quite evident." This also helps refocus the family counseling session on the child and his or her needs, rather than to focus solely on the family's experience (Goodrich & Gilbride, 2010).

In early stages of family counseling, it can be helpful for professionals to help family members explore their emotional reactions to the child's disclosure, such as feelings of fear, anger, or surprise and to help family members identify ways they can express these feelings to their child that will facilitate understanding and communication rather than judgment and rejection (Goodrich & Gilbride, 2010; Savin-Williams, 1996). Professionals can help structure discussions of feelings with the child in the session or can help parents script a way to talk to their child outside of session.

As family members work through some initial feelings, professionals can employ cognitive-behavioral techniques to explore and challenge family members' ideas and beliefs about sexuality and gender identity, what their child's disclosure means about them, and their anxieties and fears about their child (Goodrich & Gilbride, 2010). The goal of this is to help reduce negative emotions and to promote cognitive flexibility, which are associated with better outcomes for LGBTQ students and their families (Goodrich & Gilbride, 2010).

One important aspect of family counseling is psychoeducation. Families may benefit from knowing the following things about their LGBTQ child: the accepted medical and psychological views of sexuality and gender identity are that it is something one is born with and it is not a choice; it is likely that their child's sexuality or gender identity is permanent; there was nothing the parents did to "cause" this; there are many LGBTQ adults leading happy, stable, and successful lives (that include parenthood and families); and there are other families with LGBTQ children in their community (Goodrich & Gilbride, 2010; Hunter, 2007; Savin-Williams, 1996). Families might not be ready to take in all this information at once, so these topics may need to be gradually introduced throughout the counseling process. A good resource professionals can give to families is Our *Daughters & Sons: Questions & Answers for Parents of Gay, Lesbian & Bisexual People* from Parents, Families and Friends of Lesbians and Gays (PFLAG, 2011b), which can be downloaded from www.pflag.org.

In considering family diversity in counseling, professionals can guide discussions to better understand and help families clarify familial and cultural views of LGBTQ identities, including in the subcultures in which the family exists (Mosher, 2001). Families might explore how their new family identity will fit within these various contexts, how they feel about being open or not within these contexts, and how their relationships with others might or might not change (Mosher, 2001).

Similarly, religious identity is a topic to explore. Different religious organizations view sexual orientation and gender identity differently. Professionals will be in a better position to support the student and family by understanding how religion may impact a family's view. Generally, devoutly religious families may struggle more to accept their LGBTQ child, although they may also be more likely to place a high value on maintaining overall family functioning and may thus be motivated to find ways to adapt to the new family situation (Goodrich & Gilbride, 2010). By helping the family identify other times in which they had to make changes to adapt to new circumstances, professionals may be able to help families take steps toward a new understanding of their child and his/her place in the family. As previously discussed, greater flexibility is generally associated with more positive outcomes for LGBTQ students and their families (Goodrich & Gilbride, 2010; Reeves et al., 2010). A good resource for mental health professionals working with religious families is *Faith in our Families: Parents, Families and Friends Talk about Religion and Homosexuality* (PFLAG, 2011a), which can be downloaded from www.pflag.org.

Special Considerations for Families of Transgender Students

Parents of transgender youth may experience similar reactions to disclosure/discovery as parents of LGBQ youth—some will have suspected it based on their child's behavior, some will have negative feelings like shame or disappointment, and some will more easily accept it (Zamboni, 2006). Whatever the parent's reaction, there will likely be confusion about what the child is experiencing and how to proceed in getting the child help and support. Although parents of transgender students will benefit from many of the aforementioned strategies, services will need to be modified to address the unique experiences and needs of these children and families.

While helping the student and family members process the disclosure and its meaning, psychoeducation is critical, and it may take many discussions for the child and the family to understand the complexities of gender identity and gender dysphoria (Grossman & D'Augelli, 2007). Additionally, families need help managing their emotional reactions and questions about why their child is this way (Zamboni, 2006). As the child and family progress in their understanding, mental health professionals can support discussions about what next steps, if any, the child wants to take in terms of aligning his/her gender identity with external expressions of gender (see Chapter 8 for more information).

Families of transgender youth may experience an even more intense redefinition than families of LGBQ youth, especially if the child takes steps to align with his/her gender identity (Zamboni, 2006). Parents may need to go through a mourning process as they face the loss of the son or daughter they had and accept the emergence of their child in his/her new gender (Zamboni, 2006).

Promoting Community Connections

Families of LGBTQ students function better when they are connected to a supportive community (Goodrich & Gilbride, 2010; Saltzburg, 2004). It is a good idea for mental health professionals to develop a handout with information about local resources (if they exist in the surrounding communities) for parents of LGBTQ children. The final chapter of this book provides information about national and online resources for families. These may be particularly important for families living in areas without local resources and for families who may not be ready to disclose their child's identity to others in their community. Whether through local, national, or online communities, these larger networks provide families with support, knowledge, exposure, validation, and understanding, which puts families in a better position to help their LGBTQ child navigate adolescence and adulthood. A resource sheet for families of LGBTQ youth is on the CD.

Case Studies

Sarah

At the start of Mr. Martin's second meeting with Sarah's parents, he asks them what thoughts or concerns have come up since he initially spoke with them. Sarah's mother shares that she has been thinking a lot about how to talk with Sarah about her sexuality, as she wants to have an open relationship with her. Sarah's father shares that he feels uncomfortable talking with Sarah about sex in general, but wants her to feel loved and accepted. Both of them express feeling at a loss about helping her understand her sexuality, and, although they have gay and lesbian friends, they have never known anyone who was "mentally healthy" and bisexual. Mr. Martin validates their feelings, and helps them develop strategies to communicate with Sarah about her sexuality. For example, Sarah's father decides that he is going to say to Sarah, "I will always love you and support you in any way I can. If I don't always understand you, I hope you will be patient with me." To learn more about the family, Mr. Martin asks them questions about their family's religious and cultural backgrounds, and asks about how extended family members might react to Sarah's sexual orientation. Mr. Martin also explores with Sarah's parents their views of bisexuality as not being a healthy identity. They express an openness to learning more about it, but aren't sure where to begin. At the end of the meeting, Mr. Martin provides the parents with some resources to explore and says that he is available if they would like to talk more.

Javier

At the start of the family session, Mrs. Santos says to Javier's mom (with Javier in the room), "This is a time for Javier to share some of his thoughts and feelings with you. Some of it may be hard for you to hear, but I want to ask you to be thoughtful about how you respond to him. Sharing these things with you is very hard for him, but he is doing it because he loves you and wants you to understand him better. I know that you love him too, and you care about his feelings." Working from a plan that they developed in individual counseling, Javier then turns to his mother and says, "Mom, I know that you want me to be happy, and I'm only going to be happy if I can be who I am. I am gay. It's not something I chose, but it is who I am and who I am always going to be. I don't expect you to understand all of this right now, but I hope that with time you will accept me for who I am." Javier's mom spends much of the session listening and asking questions, such as, "Don't you think that if you met the right girl all this could change?" To which Javier replies assuredly, "Mom, I am gay. Nothing is going to change that." After about 30 minutes, Javier suggests that they end for the day. Mrs. Santos says, "With your permission Javier, I think it might be helpful if your mom and I talk for a few more minutes about how she feels about today. I will be sure to maintain your confidentiality." Javier agrees.

After Javier leaves, Mrs. Santos and Javier's mom sit in silence for a moment. Javier's mom says, "I didn't think this would happen to us, but this must be God's plan for our family. I just don't know how to help him right now or how to keep him safe from all the people who will hate him for being gay." Mrs. Santos responds, "Javier is still figuring out some of this too, but it will help him to know that you are on his side." She tells Javier's mom that she has some resources for her to look at that might help her understand more about Javier. Mrs. Santos ends the meeting by saying, "Today was a really good start."

Eleven

Accessing Community Resources

Reputable community and online resources provide invaluable information and connections for students, parents, and educators. The availability of online organizations and social networking sites allows youth and families to access services and supports that may not be available in local communities. Educators can find lesson plans, curricular units, and media resources that support professional development and student learning.

National agencies provide online and/or local community support to LGBTQ youth, parents of LGBTQ youth, parents who are LGBTQ and their children, and educators seeking to create safe and welcoming schools for all students and families. The agencies and groups listed here are not the only ones that may be helpful for any given area of need, therefore readers are urged to explore what additional supports and resources may be available in their region.

Gay, Lesbian, and Straight Education Network (GLSEN)

www.glsen.org

GLSEN's mission is to ensure that LGBTQ students are valued and respected in the school community by providing resources and training for educators, policy makers, students, and community leaders. Additionally, GLSEN conducts and publishes research that provides valuable information about the experiences and perspectives of LGBTQ students, LGBT parents and their children, school safety, and school climate.

For Students

GLSEN provides resources for students who need support (e.g., crisis hotline), who want to develop Gay-Straight Alliances (e.g., GLSEN Jump-Start Guide for Gay-Straight Alliances), and who want to advocate for LGBTQ students (e.g., Safe Space Kit).

For Educators

GLSEN provides multiple resources for educators to help them create supportive school and classroom climates (e.g., Back-to-School Guide for Creating LGBT Inclusive Environments), lesson plans and curriculum to engage students in discussions to promote safer schools, and a resource list of books and videos. Educators can join GLSEN's Educators Network to receive newsletters with resources and other tips.

Local Chapters

Currently, according to the GLSEN website, there are chapters in Arizona, California, Colorado, Connecticut, Florida, Kansas, Maine, Maryland, Massachusetts, Michigan, Missouri, Nebraska, Nevada, New Hampshire, New Jersey, New York, Ohio, Oregon, Pennsylvania, Tennessee, Texas, Virginia, and Washington, D.C.

Children of Lesbians and Gays Everywhere (COLAGE)

www.colage.org
    COLAGE is an organization created by and designed to support children and adults with parents who are LGBTQ. The mission of COLAGE is to create a world in which all kinds of families are valued and appreciated.

For Students

COLAGE provides several resources for students who have parents who are LGBTQ. On the website, there is a section for students to submit drawings and videos of their families, as well as more traditional resources, such as information for children of transgender parents and guides for youth activism. Additionally, COLAGE ran a camp for students with LGBTQ parents in 2011.

For Parents

Many resources for LGBTQ parents are available on the COLAGE website, including information regarding how to disclose to children, information about insemination and donor parenting, and lists of books regarding LGBTQ parenting and families.

For Educators

One of the best films for educators to watch regarding LGBTQ-parented families is *In My Shoes: Stories of Youth with LGBT Parents* (2005; discussed in Chapter 9). This film was produced by COLAGE and is available to watch on their website.

Parents, Family, and Friends of Lesbians and Gays (PFLAG)

www.pflag.org

PFLAG is an organization open to all (LGBTQ and allies) desiring equal rights for all people. Their goals include providing information, ending discrimination, and forming a society that embraces all aspects of diversity. Although PFLAG is a national organization, it places great emphasis on the personal connections and supports available from its many local chapters.

For Students

PFLAG offers a student scholarship program, and information about scholarships available from their national site and local chapters is available online.

For Parents

PFLAG has information both for parents of LGBTQ children as well as parents who are LGBTQ. Additionally, their *Safe Schools for All* program (see below) includes information for parents regarding advocacy and steps parents can take in helping to create safe educational environments for their children.

For Educators

This organization is committed to ensuring that schools are safe for students who are LGBTQ as well as students with parents who are LGBTQ. Their Safe Schools for All initiative involves several aspects, including a training program (*Cultivating Respect*) that can be requested in local community chapters or schools. It also provides a series of documents titled *10*

Ways to Make Schools Safer ... For All Students that provide
information such as facts about LGBTQ persons, suggestions
for policy development, and resources for teacher trainings.

Local Chapters

PFLAG has over 200 local chapters, including at least one in
every state. Their website also includes information regarding
how to start a chapter, resources for current chapters, and a
search engine to locate the closest chapter.

Human Rights Campaign (HRC)

www.hrc.org
   HRC is a national civil rights organization with over one
million members. The mission of this organization is to advocate for equal rights for all people, including LGBTQ individuals. HRC headquarters are in Washington, D.C., and this
organization actively supports political candidates who advocate for LGBTQ rights.

For Students

HRC provides information regarding the disclosure process.
Their website also provides links to numerous youth support
resources, including suicide prevention programs. Additionally, HRC supports a weekly video newsletter (*Queerly Speaking*) for LGBTQ youth, and offers annual *Generation Equality*
scholarships.

For Parents

HRC provides information regarding many issues related to
parenthood for LGBTQ individuals, including adoption, sur-
rogacy, legal rights, and custody. HRC also posts information
regarding current state and federal laws and regulations and
advocacy efforts regarding all aspects of life for LGBTQ adults,
including religion, aging, employment issues, medical and
health issues, marriage equality, and international rights and
recognition of LGBTQ persons.

For Educators

HRC created the *Welcoming Schools* program (discussed in
Chapters 5 and 9), which is available through their website.

Welcoming Schools is a comprehensive program for elementary-aged students, and includes information and guidance for teacher and staff training, policy development, and classroom exercises. Lessons are available on the CD (included in materials for Chapter 5).

Local Chapters

Currently, according to the HRC website, there are local steering committees in Arizona, California, Colorado, Connecticut, Florida, Georgia, Illinois, Kansas, Louisiana, Maine, Maryland, Massachusetts, Michigan, Minnesota, Missouri, Nevada, New York, North Carolina, Ohio, Oregon, Pennsylvania, Tennessee, Texas, Utah, Washington, and Washington, D.C. Additionally, HRC provides information regarding laws, policies, campaign issues, and other regional news items for each state, as well as information regarding other state and regional advocacy groups (e.g., Lambda Legal Chapters) for states without HRC steering committees.

Safe Schools Coalition

www.safeschoolscoalition.org

Based in Washington state, the Safe Schools Coalition compiles resources focused on helping schools (both in the United States and internationally) become safe places for all students, families, and educators, regardless of sexual orientation or gender identity. The Safe Schools Coalition also offers workshops and trainings for school staff.

For Students

The Safe School Coalition offers a collection of resources for students, including a list of hotlines, information for LGBTQ youth who are homeless or in foster care, and social networking sites.

For Educators

The Safe Schools Coalition provides many resources for teachers at different levels (e.g., elementary, middle, and high school) and of different subjects (e.g., health, history, music), including sample lesson plans, videos, and links to other websites. Additionally, teachers can download or purchase posters and stickers to post in their classrooms to indicate their inclusiveness of LGBTQ people.

American Civil Liberties Union (ACLU)

www.aclu.org/lgbt-rights

The ACLU is an organization dedicated to ensuring the civil rights (e.g., freedom of speech, equal protection, due process, and privacy) of all Americans. Formed in 1920, the ACLU has over 500,000 members and has been actively involved in campaigns and court cases that defend and ensure equal application of laws and rights for all persons.

For Students

The ACLU website provides a wealth of resources for LGBTQ students. They have links to a separate site (Get Busy, Get Equal), with information for students regarding their rights in educational settings, how to start Gay-Straight Alliances (GSAs), and other ideas for how to become active in creating safe schools and equal opportunities. Also on the website are fact sheets regarding key issues for LGBTQ students, such as prom, website filtering, and freedom of speech issues. Additionally, the ACLU provides support for students who need legal assistance with bullying, harassment, or discrimination in schools (an online submission form is available, and there is also a phone number [212-549-2673] exclusively for LGBTQ students requesting legal assistance).

For Educators

The *Library for LGBT Youth & Schools* portion of the ACLU website contains a wide variety of information that could be helpful for educators. Examples include case summaries of lawsuits involving LGBTQ students and school districts (organized by topic), as well as a series of *Letters to School Officials* on topics such as bullying and harassment, web filtering, LGBT student privacy, GSA information, and the Day of Silence (included on the CD in Chapters 4 and 7).

Local Chapters

In addition to the website, the ACLU is active on social media platforms such as Facebook and Twitter. Students, parents, and educators can also receive information or participate in discussions on hosted blog spaces. In addition, there are staffed ACLU offices in all 50 states and Washington, D.C.

Groundspark

http://groundspark.org

Groundspark is an organization that makes and distributes films to promote social change. The Respect for All Project includes a number of films focused on gender and sexual orientation. These films might be used as part of professional development with teachers and as part of integrated curriculum for students to promote awareness and acceptance.

- *Straightlaced*—This film documents the lives and struggles of teens across the sexuality and gender spectrum.
- *Let's Get Real*—Recommended for students in fifth to ninth grade, this film documents diverse students' experiences of harassment and bullying. A curriculum guide is available for this film.
- *That's a Family*—Recommended for students in K to eighth grade, this film explores diverse families. A discussion and teaching guide is available for this film.
- *It's Elementary*—This film helps teach adults how to talk with children about LGBT people, family diversity, stereotyping, and harassment.
- *It's STILL Elementary*—This film documents the impact of *It's Elementary* and follows up with students and teachers featured in the original film.
- *Celebrating the Life of Del Martin*—This film highlights the life and accomplishments of Del Martin, an activist for LGBT rights.
- *One Wedding and … a Revolution*—This film documents the political and social forces related to the first same-sex marriages in San Francisco.
- *Choosing Children*—This film explores ways that lesbian women take on parenthood (e.g., adoption, pregnancy).

The Trevor Project

www.thetrevorproject.org

The Trevor Project is an organization whose mission is to eliminate LGBTQ youth suicide. To this end, the project provides online information and social networking, as well as a

crisis call center that is available 24 hours a day, 7 days a week
(866-488-7386).

For Students

In addition to the immediate assistance provided by the hotline described above, the Trevor Project includes several ave-
nues through which youth can receive non-urgent support or
assistance. For example, students can submit questions to *Dear
Trevor*, or chat online on *TrevorChat*. The Trevor Project also
includes an exclusive social network, through which youth
can connect with peers nationwide (www.trevorspace.org).

It Gets Better Project

www.itgetsbetter.org

The It Gets Better Project was started by columnist and
LGBT activist Dan Savage, who posted a video in response to
recent suicides of LGBTQ youth. In his message, Dan and his
partner urged students to recognize that in spite of difficult
teenage years, their lives will get better. This video sparked
the submission of thousands of like-minded videos from
LGBTQ adults as well as celebrities, entertainers, athletes, and
politicians (LGBTQ and heterosexual) who all provide their
own messages of hope and tell youth that they will be valued,
respected, loved, and will have a chance to be an accepted
part of a community. In 2011, a book containing these messages was published, and the website continues to add new
submissions.

For Students

The video messages available to watch on the It Gets Better
website all speak directly to LGBTQ students. Additionally,
the website provides links to the Trevor Project (described
above) and urges youth considering suicide to call for help.

Gay Straight Alliance (GSA) Network

www.gsanetwork.org

The GSA Network is an organization dedicated to creating and supporting LGBTQ and ally youth who create or join
GSAs. In supporting school-based GSAs, the Network aims to
end isolation of LGBTQ students, develop leadership skills in

members, and make schools safer for all students. The GSA Network is based in California, although similar sites and networks are available in many other states (see below).

For Students

Supporting students is the priority and mission of the GSA Network. The website provides information for students regarding what GSAs are and how to create them, as well as ideas for GSA activities and suggestions for school-based activism. This organization also allows youth involved in GSAs to network with other clubs and provides ideas to share resources, strategies, and build supportive networks. Additionally, the GSA Network provides various supports for leadership development, including conferences, workshops, camps, and summits.

For Educators

The GSA Network provides many resources for staff members who are or aspire to become GSA advisors. These include tips on motivating students and staff to advocate for equal treatment and safety of LGBTQ students, working with resistance or hostility from staff, administration, or parents, and more general leadership skills such as transitioning to a new leader without disrupting momentum or cohesion.

Local Chapters

According to the GSA Network website, currently, there are local chapters in Alabama, Arizona, California, Colorado, Connecticut, Florida, Georgia, Illinois, Indiana, Iowa, Maine, Massachusetts, Minnesota, Mississippi, Missouri, New Jersey, New Mexico, New York, North Carolina, Ohio, Oregon, Pennsylvania, Rhode Island, South Carolina, Tennessee, Texas, Utah, Vermont, Virginia, Wisconsin, Washington, and Washington, D.C.

Encouraging Connection

There is an incredible wealth of information available to us about LGBTQ individuals and issues. Whether in person or online, students, families, and educators can get support and advice, find resources, and share ideas. Those highlighted in this chapter represent only a fraction of what is out there. However, with so many options, we must be critical consumers and ensure that the information we provide to students and families is accurate and meaningful. There is a resource guide for LGBTQ youth on the CD.

Case Studies

Sarah

After learning about the GSA Network from her social studies teacher, Sarah does some online research and finds her local chapter in New York. Although her school does not have a GSA, she is interested in attending their youth activism workshops, particularly *Activism 101*. Sarah attends this workshop with a few of her classmates, and they decide to work at the high school she will be attending in the fall to establish a GSA. Additionally, Sarah finds the *Queerly Speaking* video newsletters posted on the Human Rights Campaign website, and is inspired by the active roles played by LGBTQ youth nationwide. She and her friends begin filming their experiences in forming a GSA in New York City, and hope to have their video published on the *Queerly Speaking* website in the fall.

Following up on a suggestion by Mr. Martin, Sarah's parents begin exploring the resources and materials provided on the PFLAG website. They found the *Our Daughters and Sons: Questions and Answers for Parents of Lesbian, Gay, and Bisexual People* pamphlet very helpful. In discussing PFLAG, Sarah's parents agree that they would not feel comfortable attending community meetings with parents they do not know, even if these parents also have children who are LGBTQ. Instead, they decide that they prefer to continue to gather information about bisexuality online and through books, utilizing one another for support.

Javier

A few days after her meeting with Mrs. Santos, Javier's mom brings out the brochures that Mrs. Santos gave her. One was a short handout listing facts and myths about LGBTQ people, created by the Human Rights Campaign. On the list were thoughts and ideas that she recognized, including the idea that sexual orientation is a choice, or that people who are LGBTQ can change. Although she had already discussed these concepts with Mrs. Santos, it was comforting to review this information in private, to read additional explanations about what it means to be LGBTQ, and to be assured that many of her plans regarding Javier's future can still come true, including him having a healthy relationship, becoming a parent, and leading a happy life.

Another brochure that Javier's mother received from Mrs. Santos contained information about the Dallas chapter of Parents, Families, and Friends of Lesbians and Gays (PFLAG). After reviewing the information provided in the brochure, she goes online and begins to explore their website. She reads several stories written by parents that describe their experiences in learning about their son's or daughter's sexual orientation, as well as their connection and involvement with PFLAG. She is surprised to learn that there is a group of parents with LGBTQ children who meet monthly in Dallas, and that there is a list of books and materials that she can borrow from the PFLAG library, including several titles that look interesting to her. Javier's mother completes and submits an online application for membership in PFLAG. She decides that although she cannot yet discuss Javier's sexual orientation with his father, it will be helpful if she can talk to *someone* about it. Her hope for when she attends the PFLAG meeting is that she can find one or two mothers who have been through similar experiences that she can relate to and share her feelings.

References

A.B. 9, 2011 Leg., Reg. Sess. (CA, 2011).

Ali, R. (2010). *Dear colleague letter.* Retrieved from the United States Department of Education, Office of Civil Rights website: http://www2.ed.gov/about/offices/list/ocr/letters/colleague-201010.pdf

American Civil Liberties Union. (2006). *Speaking out with your t-shirt. A quick guide for lesbian, gay, bisexual, and transgender high school students.* Retrieved from the American Civil Liberties Union website: http://www.aclu.org/files/pdfs/lgbt/schoolsyouth/speakingoutwithyourtshirt.pdf

American Civil Liberties Union. (2011). *Know your prom rights! A quick guide for LGBT high school students.* Retrieved from the American Civil Liberties Union website: http://www.aclu.org/lgbt-rights/know-your-prom-night-rights-quick-guide-lgbt-high-school-students

Athanases, S. Z. (1996). A gay-themed lesson in an ethnic literature curriculum: Tenth graders' responses to "Dear Anita." *Harvard Educational Review, 66*(2), 231–256. Retrieved from http://www.hepg.org/main/her/Index.html

Athanases, S. Z. (1999). Building cultural diversity into the literature curriculum. In E. R. Hollins & E. I. Oliver (Eds.), *Pathways to success in school: Culturally responsive teaching* (pp. 139–155). Mahwah, NJ: Erlbaum.

Auslander, B. A., Rosenthal, S. L., & Blythe, M. J. (2006). Sexual development and behaviors of adolescents. *Psychiatric Annals, 36*(10), 694–702. Retrieved from http://www.psychiatricannalsonline.com/view.asp?rid=20793

Bauman, S. (2011). *Cyberbullying: What counselors need to know.* Alexandria, VA: American Counseling Association.

Bauman, S., & Sachs-Kapp, P. (1998). A school takes a stand: Promotion of sexual orientation workshops by counselors. *Professional School Counseling, 1*(3), 42–45. Retrieved from http://schoolcounselor.metapress.com/home/main.mpx

Beane, A. (2005). *The bully free classroom: Over 100 tips and strategies for teachers K-8.* Minneapolis, MN: Free Spirit Publishing.

Bechard, M. (1999). *If it doesn't kill you.* New York, NY: Viking.

Bedell, J. (2003). Personal liability of school officials under §1983 who ignore peer harassment of gay students. *Illinois Law Review, 3,* 829–862. Retrieved from http://illinois-lawreview.org/wp-content/ilr-content/articles/2003/3/Bedell.pdf

Ben-Ari, A. (1995). The discovery that an offspring is gay: Parents', gay men's, and lesbians' perspectives. *Journal of Homosexuality, 30*(1), 89-112. doi:10.1300/J082v30n01_05

Birkett, M., Espelage, D. L., & Koenig, B. (2009). LGB and questioning students in schools: The moderating effects of homophobic bullying and school climate on negative outcomes. *Journal of Youth Adolescence, 38,* 989–1000. doi:10.1007/s10964-008-9389-1

Blake, S. M., Ledsky, R., Lehman, T., Goodenow, C., Sawyer, R., & Hack, T. (2001). Preventing sexual risk behaviors among gay, lesbian, and bisexual adolescents: The benefits of gay-sensitive HIV instruction in schools. *American Journal of Public Health, 91*(6), 940–946. Retrieved from http://ajph.aphapublications.org/

Brummel, B. (Producer), Rhode, J. (Director) & Newfield, J. (Director). (2010). *Bullied: A student, a school, and a case that made history* [Motion Picture]. United States: Teaching Tolerance.

Bryan, J. (2010, Summer). From the dress-up corner to the senior prom: Navigating gender & sexual identity development in schools. *Independent School, 69*(4), 42–47.

Burn, S., Kadlec, K., & Rexer, R. (2005). Effects of subtle heterosexism on gays, lesbians, and bisexuals. *Journal of Homosexuality, 49*(2), 23–38. doi:10.1300/J082v49n02_02

Burns, K. (2007). Giving voice, making change: How PFLAG resources can be useful classroom tools. *Journal of Gay & Lesbian Issues in Education, 4*(2), 107–109. doi:10.1300/J367v04n02_10

Chick, K. (2008). Fostering an appreciation for all kinds of families: Picturebooks with gay and lesbian themes. *Bookbird: A Journal of International Children's Literature, 46*(1), 15–22. doi:10.1353/bkb.0.0013

Children of Lesbians and Gays Everywhere [COLAGE] Youth Leadership and Action Program (Producer), & Gilomen, J.

(Director) (2005). *In my shoes: Stories of youth with LGBT parents* [Motion Picture]. United States: COLAGE.

Cohen, H. (Producer), Chasnoff, D. (Producer), & Chasnoff, D. (Director). (1996). *Its Elementary: Talking about gay issues in school* [Motion Picture]. United States: Women's Educational Media.

Colapinto, J. (2000). *As nature made him: The boy who was raised as a girl.* New York, NY: HarperCollins.

Committee for Children. (2010). *Second Step: Skills for social and academic success.* Seattle, WA: Author.

Committee for Children. (2001). *Steps to Respect: A bullying prevention program.* Seattle, WA: Author.

Cooper-Nicols, M., & Bowleg, L. (2010). "My voice is being heard": Exploring the experiences of gay, lesbian, and bisexual youth in schools. In C. Bertram, M. Crowley, & S. Massey (Eds.), *Beyond progress and marginalization: LGBTQ youth in educational contexts* (pp. 15–51). New York, NY: Peter Lang.

Cowie, H., & Rivers, I. (2000). Going against the grain: Supporting lesbian, gay and bisexual clients as they 'come out'. *British Journal of Guidance & Counselling, 28*(4), 503–513. doi:10.1080/03069880020004712

Crothers, L. (2007). Bullying of sexually diverse children and adolescents. *NASP Communique, 35*(5), 28–30. Retrieved from http://www.nasponline.org/publications/cq/mocq 355bullying.aspx

Cuijpers, P. (2002). Peer-led and adult-led school drug prevention: A meta-analytic comparison. *Journal of Drug Education, 32*(2), 107–119. doi:10.2190/LPN9-KBDC-HPVB-JPTM

Daniel, P. (2007). Invitation to all: Welcoming gays and lesbians into my classroom and curriculum. *The English Journal, 95*(5), 75–80. Retrieved from http://www.jstor.org/stable/30046715

D'Augelli, A. R., Grossman, A., & Starks, M. (2008). Families of gay, lesbian, and bisexual youth: What do parents and siblings know and how do they react? *Journal of GLBT Family Studies, 4*(1), 95–115. doi:10.1080/15504280802084506

D'Augelli, A. R., Hershberger, S. L., & Pilkington, N. W. (1998). Lesbian, gay, and bisexual youth and their families: Disclosure of sexual orientation and its consequences. *American Journal of Orthopsychiatry, 68*(3), 361–371. doi:10.1037/h0080345

DeBord, K. A., & Perez, R. M. (2000). Group counseling theory and practice with lesbian, gay, and bisexual clients. In R.

M. Perez, K. A. DeBord, & K. J. Bieschke (Eds.), *Handbook of counseling and psychotherapy with lesbian, gay, and bisexual clients* (pp. 183–206). doi:10.1037/10339-008

de Haan, L., & Nijland, S. (2000). *King & king*. Berkeley, CA: Tricycle Press.

de Haan, L., & Nijland, S. (2004*). King & king & family*. Berkeley, CA: Tricycle Press.

DeNies, Y., James, S., & Netter, S. (2010). Mean girls: Cyberbullying named for teen suicide. *Good Morning America, abcnews. com*. Retrieved from http://abcnews.go.com/GMA/Parenting/girls-teen-suicide-calls-attention-cyberbullying/story?id=9685026

DeLamater, J., & Friedrich, W. N. (2002). Human sexual development. *The Journal of Sex Research, 39*(1), 10–14. Retrieved from http://www.informaworld.com/smpp/title~content=t775653667

Denny, D., & Pittman, C. (2009). Gender identity: From dualism to diversity. In M. S. Tepper & A. Fuglsang Owens (Eds.), *Sexual health: Psychological foundations* (Vol. 1, pp. 205–229). Westport, CT: Praeger.

Diamond, L. M., & Butterworth, M. (2008). The close relationships of sexual minorities: Partners, friends and family. In C. M. Smith & N. DeFrates-Densch (Eds.), *Handbook of research on adult learning and development* (pp. 351–377). New York, NY: Routledge/Taylor & Francis Group.

Draughn, T., Elkins, B., & Roy, R. (2002). Allies in the struggle: Eradicating homophobia and heterosexism on campus. *Journal of Lesbian Studies, 6*(3/4), 9–20. Retrieved from http:///www.tandf.co.uk/journals/WJLS

Dworkin, S. H. (2000). Individual therapy with lesbian, gay, and bisexual clients. In R. M. Perez, K. A. DeBord, & K. J. Bieschke (Eds.), *Handbook of counseling and psychotherapy with lesbian, gay, and bisexual clients* (pp. 157–181). doi:10.1037/10339-007

Eckholm, E. W. (2011). In isolated Utah city, new clubs for gay students. *New York Times*. Retrieved from http://www.nytimes.com

Espelage, D. L., Aragon, S. R., Birkett, M., & Koenig, B. W. (2008). Homophobic teasing, psychological outcomes, and sexual orientation among high school students: What influence do parents and schools have? *School Psychology Review, 37*(2), 202–216. Retrieved from http://www.nasponline.org/publications/spr/pdf/spr372espelage.pdf

Esseks, J. (2009). Letter to school principals and educators about school censorship. Retrieved from the American Civil Liberties Union website: http://www.aclu.org/free-speech/letter-principals-and-educators-about-school-censorship

Esseks, J. (2010). *Letter to school officials about addressing anti-LGBT bullying.* Retrieved from the American Civil Liberties Union website: http://www.aclu.org/lgbt-rights/letter-school-officials-about-addressing-anti-lgbt-bullying

Esseks, J. (2011). *Letter to school officials regarding gay/straight alliances.* Retrieved from the American Civil Liberties Union website: http://www.aclu.org/lgbt-rights_hiv-aids/letter-school-officials-regarding-gaystraight-alliances

Family Equality Council. (2008). Opening doors: Lesbian, gay, bisexual, and transgender (LGBT) parents and schools. Retrieved from the Family Equality Council website: http://www.familyequality.org/pdf/openingdoors.pdf

Fassinger, R. E. (2000). Applying counseling theories to lesbian, gay, and bisexual clients: Pitfalls and possibilities. In R. M. Perez, K. A. DeBord, & K. J. Bieschke (Eds.), *Handbook of counseling and psychotherapy with lesbian, gay, and bisexual clients* (pp. 107–131). doi:10.1037/10339-005

Fisher, E. S., Komosa-Hawkins, K., Saldaña, E., Thomas, G. M., Hsiao, C., Rauld, M., & Miller, D. (2008). Promoting school success for lesbian, gay, bisexual, transgendered, and questioning students: Primary, secondary, and tertiary prevention and intervention strategies. *The California School Psychologist, 13,* 79–91. Retrieved from http://www.caspsurveys.org/NEW/pdfs/journal08.pdf#page=79

Fisher, E. S., & Thomas, G. (2009). Culturally sensitive classroom management and positive behavior support in secondary schools. In E. F. Litton & S. P. Martin (Eds.), *Justice, care and diversity: Addressing the needs of all students in Catholic secondary schools* (pp. 138–154). Washington, DC: National Catholic Educational Association.

Flores v. Morgan Hill Unified School District, 324 F.3d 1130 (9th Cir. 2003)

Fox, R. (2007). One of the hidden diversities in schools: Families with parents who are lesbian or gay. *Childhood Education, 83,* 277–281. Retrieved from http://www.tandf.co.uk/journals/UCED

Friedlander, W. (2011). Gay and lesbian characters are popping up on shows for young people. *Los Angeles Times.* Retrieved from http://www.latimes.com

Galambos, N. L., Berenbaum, S. A., & McHale, S. M. (2009). Gender development in adolescence. In R. M. Lerner & L. Steinberg (Eds.), *Handbook of adolescent psychology: Individual bases of adolescent development* (3rd ed., Vol. 1, pp. 305–357). Hoboken, NJ; Wiley.

Garden, N. (1999). *The year they burned the books.* New York, NY: Farrar, Straus & Giroux.

Garden, N. (2000). *Holly's secret.* New York, NY: Farrar, Straus & Giroux.

Garden, N. (2004). *Molly's family.* New York, NY: Farrar, Straus & Giroux.

Garmezy, N. (1993). Children in poverty: Resilience despite risk. *Psychiatry, 56,* 127–136.

Garnets, L., Hancock, K. A., Cochran, S. D., Goodchilds, J., & Peplau, L. (1991). Issues in psychotherapy with lesbians and gay men: A survey of psychologists. *American Psychologist, 46*(9), 964–972. doi:10.1037/0003-066X.46.9.964

Gastic, B., & Johnson, D. (2009). Teacher-mentors and the educational resilience of sexual minority youth. *Journal of Gay & Lesbian Social Services, 21,* 219–231. doi: 10.1080/10538720902772139

Gay, Lesbian, and Straight Education Network (GLSEN). (2004). Student survey: Name calling and verbal bullying. Retrieved from the GLSEN website: http://www. nonamecallingweek.org/binary-data/NoNameCalling_ ATTACHMENTS/file/13-1.pdf

Gay-Straight Alliance Network, Transgender Law Center, & the National Center for Lesbian Rights (2004). *Beyond the binary: A tool kit for gender identity activism in schools.* Retrieved from the Gay-Straight Alliance Network website: http://www.gsanetwork.org/files/getinvolved/Beyondthe Binary-Manual.pdf

Gilley, J. W. (2004). Demonstration and simulation. In M. W. Galbraith (Ed.), *Adult learning methods: A guide for effective instruction* (pp. 361–381). Malabar, FL: Krieger.

Goldstein, A. (1999). *The PREPARE curriculum.* Champaign, IL: Research Press.

Gonzalez, R. (2005). *Antonio's card.* San Francisco, CA: Children's Book Press.

Goodrich, C., & Luke, M. (2009). LGBTQ responsive school counseling. *Journal of LGBT Issues in Counseling, 3,* 113–127. doi:10.1080/15538600903005284

Goodrich, K. M., & Gilbride, D. D. (2010). The refinement and validation of a model of a family functioning after child's disclosure as lesbian, gay, or bisexual. *Journal of LGBT Issues in Counseling, 4*(2), 92–121. doi:10.1080/15538605.2010.483575

Gordon, S. (2000). *All families are different*. Amherst, NY: Prometheus Books.

Graybill, E., Varjas, K., Meyers, J., & Watson, L. (2009). Content-specific strategies to advocate for lesbian, gay, bisexual, and transgender youth: An exploratory study. *School Psychology Review, 38*(4), 570–584. Retrieved from http://www.nasponline.org/publications/spr/sprissues.aspx

Greenbaum, V. (1994). Literature out of the closet: Bringing gay and lesbian texts and subtexts out in high school English. *The English Journal, 83*(5), 71–74. Retrieved from http://www.jstor.org/stable/820418

Greytak, E. A., Kosciw, J. G., & Diaz, E. M. (2009). *Harsh realities: The experiences of transgender youth in our nation's schools.* Retrieved from the Gay, Lesbian, and Straight Education Network website: http://www.glsen.org/binary-data/GLSEN_ATTACHMENTS/file/000/001/1375-1.pdf

Grossman, A. H., & D'Augelli, A. R. (2007). Transgender youth and life-threatening behaviors. *Suicide and Life-Threatening Behaviors, 37*(5), 527–537. doi:10.1521/suli.2007.37.5.527

Hansen, A. (2007). School-based support for GLBT students: A review of three levels of research. *Psychology in the Schools, 44,* 839–848. doi:10.1002/pits20269

Hartinger, B. (2007). *Split screen: Attack of the soul-sucking brain zombies/bride of the soul- sucking brain zombies.* New York, NY: HarperCollins.

Heatherington, L., & Lavner, J. A. (2008). Coming to terms with coming out: Review and recommendations for family systems-focused research. *Journal of Family Psychology, 22*(3), 329–343. doi:10.1037/0893-3200.22.3.329

Henkle v. Gregory, 150 F.Supp. 2d 1067 (D. Nev., 2001)

Hillier, L. (2002). "It's a catch-22": Same-sex attracted young people on coming out to parents. In S. S. Feldman & D. Rosenthal (Eds.), *Talking sexuality: Parent-adolescent communication* (pp. 75–91). San Francisco, CA: Jossey-Bass.

Hirschstein, M., Edstrom, L., Frey, K., Snell, J., & MacKenzie, E. (2007). Walking the talk in bullying prevention: Teacher implementation variables related to initial impact of the Steps to Respect Program. *School Psychology Review, 36,*

3–21. Retrieved from http://www.nasponline.org/publications/spr/sprissues.aspx

Hoffman, E. (1999). *Best best colors (los mejores colores)*. Saint Paul, MN: Redleaf Press.

Hollins, E. R. (1999). Becoming a reflective practitioner. In E. R. Hollins & E. I. Oliver (Eds.), *Pathways to success in school: Culturally responsive teaching* (pp. 11–33). Mahwah, NJ: Erlbaum.

Holmes, S., & Cahill, S. (2004). School experiences of gay, lesbian, bisexual and transgender youth. *Journal of Gay & Lesbian Issues in Education, 1*(13), 53–66. doi:10.1300/J367v01n03_06

Horn, S., Kosciw, J., & Russell, S. (2009). Special issue introduction: New research on lesbian, gay, bisexual, and transgender youth: Studying lives in context. *Journal of Youth and Adolescence, 38,* 863–866. doi:10.1007/s10964-009-9420-1

Hornor, G. (2004). Sexual behavior in children: Normal or not? *Journal of Pediatric Health Care, 18*(2), 57–64. doi:10/1016/S0891-5245(03)00154-8

Human Rights Campaign (2011, April 12). Parenting laws: Joint adoption. Retrieved from http://www.hrc.org/state_laws

Human Rights Campaign. (2011, July 6). Marriage equality and other relationship recognition laws. Retrieved from http://www.hrc.org/state_laws

Human Rights Campaign. (2011, July 11). Statewide school laws and policies. Retrieved from http://www.hrc.org/state_laws

Human Rights Campaign Foundation. (2009). *Welcoming schools: An inclusive approach to addressing family diversity, gender stereotyping, and name-calling in K-5 learning environments.* Retrieved from the Human Rights Campaign website: http://www.hrc.org/issues/7201.htm

Hunter, S. (2007). *Coming out and disclosures: LGBT persons across the life span.* Binghamton, NY: The Haworth Press.

Iron Zeal Films (Producer), & Schutz, S. (Director). (2007). *Anyone and everyone* [Motion Picture]. United States: American Public Television.

Israel, T., Gorcheva, R., Burnes, T. R., & Walther, W. A. (2008). Helpful and unhelpful therapy experiences of LGBT clients. *Psychotherapy Research, 18*(3), 294–305. doi:10.1080/10503300701506920

Jeltova, I., & Fish, M. (2005). Creating school environments responsive to gay, lesbian, bisexual, and transgender families: Traditional and systemic approaches for consultation. *Journal of Educational and Psychological Consultation, 16,* 17–33. doi:10.1080/10474412.2005.9669 525

Jennett, M. (2004). Stand up for us: Challenging homophobia in schools. Retrieved from the Department for Education and Skills website: https://www.education.gov.uk/publications/eOrderingDownload/SUFU%20Final.pdf

Jennings, K. (2003). *Always my child.* New York, NY: Simon & Schuster.

Just the Facts Coalition. (2008). *Just the facts about sexual orientation and youth: A primer for principals, educators, and school personnel.* Washington, DC: American Psychological Association. Retrieved from http://www.apa.org/pi/lgbc/publications/justthefacts.html

Keen, L. (2007). *Out law: What LGBT youth should know about their legal rights.* Boston, MA: Beacon.

Kennedy, K. G., & Fisher, E. S. (2010). Bisexual students in secondary schools: Understanding unique experiences and developing responsive practices. *Journal of Bisexuality, 10*(4), 427–485. doi:10.1080/15299716.2010.521061

Knowles, M. S., Holton, E. F., III., & Swanson, R. A. (2005). *The adult learner: The definitive classic in adult education and human resource development.* Burlington, MA: Elsevier, Inc.

Koerner, M., & Hulsebosch, P. (1996). Preparing teachers to work with children of gay and lesbian parents. *Journal of Teacher Education, 47,* 347–354. doi:10.1177/0022487196047005004

Kosciw, J. G., & Diaz, E. M. (2008). *Involved, invisible, ignored: The experience of lesbian, gay, bisexual, and transgender parents and their children in our nation's K-12 schools.* Retrieved from the Gay, Lesbian, and Straight Education Network website: http://www.glsen.org/binary-data/GLSEN_ATTACHMENTS/file/000/001/1104-1.pdf

Kosciw, J. G., Greytak, E. A., & Diaz, E. M. (2009). Who, what, where, when, and why: Demographic and ecological factors contributing to hostile school climate for lesbian, gay, bisexual and transgender youth. *Journal of Youth and Adolescence, 38,* 976–988. doi:10.1007/s10964-009-9412-1

Kosciw, J. G., Greytak, E. A., Diaz, E. M., & Bartkiewicz, M. J. (2010). The 2009 national school climate survey: The experiences of lesbian, gay, bisexual and transgender youth in our nation's schools. Retrieved from the Gay,

Lesbian, and Straight Education Network website: http://www.glsen.org/binarydata/GLSEN_ATTACHMENTS/file/000/001/1675-2.pdf

Kozik-Rosabal, G. (2000). "Well, we haven't noticed anything bad going on," said the principal: Parents speak out about their gay families and schools. *Education and Urban Society, 32*, 368–389. doi:10.1177/0013124500323006

Lambda Legal (2000, January). *Henkle v. Gregory.* Retrieved from http://www.lambdalegal.org/in-court/cases/henkle-v-gregory.html

Larney, M. (2009). *LGBT youth human rights: Protecting the human rights of LGBT American secondary school students.* Köln, Germany: Lambert Academic Publishing.

Lennon, E., & Mistler, B. J. (2010). Breaking the binary: Providing effective counseling to transgender students in college and university settings. *Journal of LGBT Issues in Counseling, 4*(3–4), 228–240. doi:10.1080/15538605.2010.524848

Lesbian and Gay Parents Association of San Francisco (Producer, Director). (1994). *Both my moms' names are Judy: Children of lesbians and gays speak out* [Motion Picture]. United States: Lesbian and Gay Parents Association of San Francisco.

Lev, A. (2006). Intersexuality in the family: An unacknowledged trauma. *Journal of Gay & Lesbian Psychotherapy, 10(2)*, 26–56. doi:0.1300/J236v10n02_03

Liddle, B. J. (1996). Therapist sexual orientation, gender, and counseling practices as they relate to ratings on helpfulness by gay and lesbian clients. *Journal of Counseling Psychology, 43*(4), 394–401. doi:10.1037/0022-0167.43.4.394

Lieberman, R., Poland, S., & Cassel, R. (2008). Best practices in suicide intervention. In A. Thomas & J. Grimes (Eds.), *Best practices in school psychology* (Vol. 5, pp. 1457–1472). Bethesda, MD: NASP Publications.

Linville, D., & Carlson, D. L. (2010). Fashioning sexual selves: Examining the care of self in urban adolescent sexuality and gender disclosures. *Journal of LGBT Youth, 7*(3), 247–261. Retrieved from http://www.tandf.co.uk/journals/WJLY

Lo, M. (2009). *Ash.* New York, NY: Little, Brown and Company.

Lovett, I. (2011, July 14). California to require gay history in schools. *New York Times.* Retrieved from http://www.nytimes.com

MacKenzie, D., Huntington, A., & Gilmour, J. A. (2009). The experiences of people with an intersex condition: A journey from silence to voice. *Journal of Clinical Nursing, 18,* 1775–1783. doi:10.1111/j.1365-2702.2008.02710.x

Malley, M., & Tasker, F. (2007). "The difference that makes a difference": What matters to lesbians and gay men in psychotherapy. *Journal of Gay & Lesbian Psychotherapy, 11*(1), 93–109. doi:10.1300/J236v11n01_07

Marshall, M., Friedman, M., Stall, R., King, K., Miles, J., Gold, M., … Morse, J. Sexual orientation and adolescent substance use: A meta-analysis and methodological review. *Addiction, 103,* 546–556. doi:10.1111/j.1360-0443.2008.02149.x

Martin, K. A., Hutson, D. J., Kazyak, E., & Scherrer, K. S. (2010). Advice when children come out: The cultural "tool kits" of parents. *Journal of Family Issues, 123*(1), 346–352. doi:10.1177/01925X09354454

Mason, H. (2003, September). *Peer education: Promoting healthy behaviors.* Advocates For Youth. Retrieved from http://www.advocatesforyouth.org

Mathison, C. (1998). The invisible minority: Preparing teachers to meet the needs of gay and lesbian youth. *Journal of Teacher Education, 49,* 151–155. doi: 10.1177/0022487198049002008

Matteson, D. R. (1996). Counseling and psychotherapy with bisexual and exploring clients. In B. A. Firestein (Ed.), *Bisexuality: The psychology and politics of an invisible minority* (pp. 185–213). Thousand Oaks, CA: Sage.

Maurer, L. (2009). Out of the closet and into the classroom: Including sexual orientation and gender identity in teaching sexuality. In E. Schroeder & J. Kuriansky (Eds.), *Sexuality education: Past, present, and future* (Vol. 3, pp., 354–389,). Westport, CT: Praeger.

Mayberry, M. (2006). The story of a Salt Lake City Gay-Straight Alliance: Identity work and LGBT youth. *Journal of Gay & Lesbian Issues in Education, 4*(1), 13–31. doi:10.1300/J367v04n01_03

McGuire, J., Anderson, C., Toomey, R., & Russell, S. (2010). School climate for transgender youth: A mixed-method investigation of student experiences and school responses. *Journal of Youth and Adolescence, 39,* 1175–1188. doi:10.1007/s10964-010-9540-7

McNaught, B. (1988). *Dear Anita: Late night thoughts of an Irish Catholic homosexual.* New York, NY: St. Martin's Press.

Mellanby, A. R., Newcombe, R. G., Rees, J., & Tripp, J. H. (2001). A comparative study of peer-led and adult-led school sex education. *Health Education Research, 16*(4), 481–492. doi:10.1093/her/16.4.481

Miller, D. N., & Eckert, T. L. (2009). Youth suicidal behavior: An introduction and overview. *School Psychology Review, 38*(2), 153–167. Retrieved from http://www.nasponline. org/publications/spr/pdf/spr382millerintro.pdf

Miller, J. L., House, R. M., & Tyler, V. (2002). Group counseling with gay, lesbian, and bisexual clients. In D. Capuzzi & D. R. Gross (Eds.), *Introduction to group counseling* (3rd ed., pp. 460–503). Denver, CO: Love Publishing.

Morgan, D. (2003). Knowledge and attitudes of preservice teachers toward students that are gay, lesbian, bisexual, or transgendered. Available from ProQuest Dissertations and Theses Database. (Umi No. AAT3117270)

Mosher, C. M. (2001). The social implications of sexual identity formation and the coming-out process: A review of the theoretical and empirical literature. *The Family Journal: Counseling and Therapy for Couples and Families, 9*(2), 164–173. doi:10.1177/1066480701092011

Mufioz-Plaza, C., Quinn, S., & Rounds, K. (2002). Lesbian, gay, bisexual and transgender students: Perceived social support in the high school environment. *The High School Journal, 85*(3), 52–63. Retrieved from http://www.jstor. org/stable/40364362

Muller, L. E., & Hartman, J. (1998). Group counseling for sexual minority youth. *Professional School Counseling, 1*(3), 38–41. Retrieved from http://schoolcounselor.metapress. com/home/main.mpx

Murdock, T. B., & Bolch, M. B. (2005). Risk and protective factors for poor school adjustment in lesbian, gay, and bisexual (LGB) high school youth: Variable and person-centered analyses. *Psychology in the Schools, 42*(2), 159–172. doi:10.1002/pits.20054

Nabozny v. Podlesny, 92 F.3d 446 (7th Cir. 1996)

Newman-Carlson, D., Horne, A., & Bartolomucci, C. (2000). *Bully Busters: A teacher's manual for helping bullies, victims, and bystanders grades 6–8.* Champaign, IL: Research Press.

Noland, R. M. (2006). Childhood sexuality and sexual behavior. In R. J. Waller (Ed.), *Fostering child and adolescent mental health in the classroom* (pp. 203–221). Thousand Oaks, CA: Sage.

Orban, L. (2003). Protective factors and psychological well-being in lesbian, gay, and bisexual youth: An ecological framework. Available from ProQuest Dissertations and Theses Database. (Umi No. AAT 3098120)

Padilla, Y. C., Crisp, C., & Rew, D. (2010). Parental acceptance and illegal drug use among gay, lesbian, and bisexual adolescents: Results from a national survey. *Social Work, 55*(3), 265–275. Retrieved from http://www.ncbi.nlm.nih.gov/pubmed/20632661

Parents, Families and Friends of Lesbians and Gays (PFLAG). (2011a). *Faith in our families: Parents, families and friends talk about religion and homosexuality* [Brochure]. Washington, D.C.

Parents, Families and Friends of Lesbians and Gays (PFLAG). (2011b). *Our daughters & sons: Questions & answers for parents of gay, lesbian & bisexual people* [Brochure]. Washington, D.C.

Parks, C. A., Hughes, T. L., & Matthews, A. K. (2004). Race/ethnicity and sexual orientation: Intersecting identities. *Cultural Diversity and Ethnic Minority Psychology, 10*(3), 241–254. doi:10.1037/1099-9809.10.3.241

Parr, T. (2003). *The family book.* New York, NY: Little, Brown & Co.

Patterson, C. J. (2000). Family relationships of lesbians and gay men. *Journal of Marriage and the Family, 62*(4), 1052–1069. doi:10.1111/j.1741-3737.2000.01052.x

Perkins, F. D. (1999). People like us: African American children respond to self-affirming texts. In E. R. Hollins & E. I. Oliver (Eds.), *Pathways to success in school: Culturally responsive teaching* (pp. 47–59). Mahwah, NJ: Erlbaum.

Pilkington, N. W., & D'Augelli, A. R. (1995). Victimization of lesbian, gay, and bisexual youth in community settings. *Journal of Community Psychology, 23*(1), 34–56. doi:10.1002/1520-6629(199501)23:1<34::AID-JCOP2290230105>3.0.CO;2-N

Pluhar, E. (2009). Childhood sexuality. In M. S. Tepper & A. Fuglsang Owens (Eds.), *Sexual health: Psychological foundations* (Vol. 1, pp. 155–181). Westport, CT: Praeger.

Pope, A. L., Mobley, A., & Myers, J. E. (2010). Integrating identities for same-sex attracted clients: Using developmental counseling and therapy to address sexual orientation conflicts. *Journal of LGBT Issues in Counseling, 4*(1), 32–47. doi:10.1080/15538600903552749

Pope, M., Bunch, L. K., Szymanski, D. M., & Rankins, M. (2004). Counseling sexual minority students in the schools. In B. T. Erford (Ed.), *Professional school counseling: A handbook of theories, programs & practices* (pp. 699–717). Austin, TX: Pro-Ed, Inc.

Poteat, V. P., Espelage, D. L., & Koenig, B. W. (2009). Willingness to remain friends and attend school with lesbian and gay peers: Relational expressions of prejudice among heterosexual youth. *Journal of Youth Adolescence, 38,* 952–962. doi:10.1007/s10964-009-9416-x

Potoczniak, D., Crosbie-Burnett, M., & Saltzburg, N. (2009). Experiences regarding coming out to parents among African American, Hispanic, and White gay, lesbian, bisexual, transgender, and questioning adolescents. *Journal of Gay & Lesbian Social Services, 21,* 189–205. doi: 10.1080/10538720902772063

Ray, N. (2006). *Lesbian, gay, bisexual and transgender youth: An epidemic of homelessness.* New York, NY: National Gay and Lesbian Task Force Policy Institute and the National Coalition for the Homeless.

Reeves, T., Horne, S. G., Rostosky, S. S., Riggle, E. D. B., Baggett, L. R., & Aycock, R. A. (2010). Family members' support for GLBT issues: The role of family adaptability and cohesion. *Journal of GLBT Family Studies, 6,* 80–97. doi: 10.1080/15504280903472857

Resnick, M., Bearman, P., Blum, R., Bauman, K., Harris, K., Jones, J., ... Udry, R. (1997). Protecting adolescents from harm: Findings from the National Longitudinal Study on Adolescent Health. *Journal of the American Medical Association, 278,* 823–832. Retrieved from http://cals-cf. calsnet.arizona.edu/fcs/bpy/spotlightArchives/1-resnick%20JAMA.pdf

Reynolds, A. L., & Hanjorgiris, W. F. (2000). Coming out: Lesbian, gay, and bisexual identity development. In R. M. Perez, K. A. DeBord, & K. J. Bieschke (Eds.), *Handbook of counseling and psychotherapy with lesbian, gay, and bisexual clients* (pp. 35–55). doi:10.1037/10339-002

Richardson, J., & Parnell, P. (2005). *And Tango makes three.* New York, NY: Simon & Schuster.

Rogers, A. & Horrocks, N. (2010). *Teaching adults (4 ed.).* New York, NY: Open University Press.

Rosario, V. A. (2006). "Is it a boy or a girl?" Introduction to special issue on intersex. *Journal of Gay & Lesbian Psychotherapy, 10*(2), 1–7. doi:10.1300/J236v10n02_01

Rosario, M., Schrimshaw, E. W., & Hunter, J. (2004). Ethnic/racial differences in the coming out process of lesbian, gay, and bisexual youths: A comparison of sexual identity development over time. *Cultural Diversity and Ethnic Minority Psychology, 10*(3), 215–228. doi:10.1037/1099-9809.10.3.215

Rosario, M., Schrimshaw, E. W., & Hunter, J. (2009). Disclosure of sexual orientation and subsequent substance use and abuse among lesbian, gay, and bisexual youths: Critical role of disclosure reactions. *Psychology of Addictive Behaviors, 23*(1), 175–184. doi:10.1037/a0014284

Rosario, M., Schrimshaw, E. W., Hunter, J., & Braun, L. (2006). Sexual identity development among lesbian, gay, and bisexual youths: Consistency and change over time. *The Journal of Sex Research, 43*(1), 46–58. doi:10.1080/00224490609552298

Russell., S. (n.d.). *Understanding and supporting lesbian, gay, bisexual, and transgender youth.* Unpublished manuscript, Norton School of Family and Consumer Sciences, University of Arizona, Tucson, Arizona.

Russell, G. M., & Bohan, J. S. (2007). Liberating psychotherapy: Liberation psychology and psychotherapy with LGBT clients. *Journal of Gay and Lesbian Psychotherapy, 11*(3), 59–75. doi:10.1300/J236v11n03_04

Russell, S. T., Seif, H., & Truong, N. L. (2001). School outcomes of sexual minority youth in the United States: Evidence from a national study. *Journal of Adolescence, 24,* 111–127. doi:10.1006/jado.2000.0365

Rutter, M. (2001). Psychosocial adversity: Risk, resilience, and recovery. In J. M. Richman & W. M. Fraser (Eds.), *The context of youth violence: Resilience, risk and protection* (pp. 13–42). Westport, CT: Praeger.

Ryan, C. (2001). Counseling lesbian, gay, and bisexual youths. In A. R. D'Augelli & C. J. Patterson (Eds.), *Lesbian, gay, and bisexual identities and youth: Psychological perspectives* (pp. 224–250). New York, NY: Oxford University Press.

Ryan, C., Russell, S., Huebner, D., Diaz, R., & Sanchez, J. (2010). Family acceptance in adolescence and the health of LGBT young adults. *Journal of Child and Adolescent Psychiatric Nursing, 23*(4), 205–213. doi:10.1111/j.1744-6171.2010.00246

Ryan, D., & Martin, A. (2000). Lesbian, gay, bisexual and transgender parents in the school systems. *School Psychol-*

ogy Review, 29(2), 207–216. Retrieved from http://www.nasponline.org/publications/spr/sprissues.aspx

Ryan, S. (2001). *Empress of the world*. New York, NY: Viking.

Sadowski, M., Chow, S., & Scanlon, C. (2009). Meeting the needs of LGBTQ youth: A relational assets approach. *Journal of LGBT Youth, 6*(2–3), 174–198. Retrieved from http://www.tandf.co.uk/journals/WJLY

Safe Schools Coalition. (n.d.). The school climate survey. Retrieved from the Safe Schools Coalition website: http://www.safeschoolscoalition.org/FreeHelpSurveyingYour-School.pdf

Safren, S., & Heimberg, R. (1999). Depression, hopelessness, suicidality, and related factors in sexual minority and heterosexual adolescents. *Journal of Consulting and Clinical Psychology, 67*, 859–866. doi:022-006X99

Salinger, J. D. (1945). *Catcher in the rye*. New York, NY: Little Brown and Company.

Saltzburg, S. (2004). Learning that an adolescent child is gay or lesbian: The parent experience. *Social Work, 49*(1), 109–118. Retrieved from http://www.broward.k12.fl.us/studentsupport/sswad/docs/LearningThatanAdolescent.pdf

Savage, D., & Miller, T. (Eds.). (2011). *It gets better: Coming out, overcoming bullying, and creating a life worth living.* New York, NY: Penguin Group.

Savin-Williams, R. C. (1990). *Gay and lesbian youth: Expressions of identity.* Washington, DC: Hemisphere Publishing.

Savin-Williams, R. C. (1994). Verbal and physical abuse as stressors in the lives of lesbian, gay male, and bisexual youths: Associations with school problems, running away, substance abuse, prostitution, and suicide. *Journal of Consulting and Clinical Psychology, 62*(2), 261–269. doi:10.1037/0022-006X.62.2.261

Savin-Williams, R. C. (1996). Self-Labeling and disclosure among gay, lesbian, and bisexual youth. In J. Laird & R. J. Green (Eds.), *Lesbians and Gays in Couples and Families* (pp. 153–182). doi:10.1037/h0080345

Savin-Williams, R. C. (2003). Lesbian, gay, and bisexual youths' relationships with their parents. In L. D. Garnets & D. C. Kimmel (Eds.), *Psychological perspectives on lesbian, gay, and bisexual experiences* (2nd ed., pp. 299–326). New York, NY: Columbia University Press.

Savin-Williams, R. (2005). *The new gay teenager.* Cambridge, MA: Harvard University Press.

Schall, J., & Kauffmann, G. (2003). Exploring literature with gays and lesbian characters in the elementary school. *Journal of Children's Literature, 29*(1), 36–45. Retrieved from http://www.childrensliteratureassembly.org/journal.html

Sexual development and behavior in children: Information for parents and caregivers. (2009, April). *The National Child Traumatic Stress Network.* Retrieved from http://www.nctsn.org

Shropshire, S. Y. (1999). Including diverse perspectives in the history curriculum. In E. R. Hollins & E. I. Oliver (Eds.), *Pathways to success in school: Culturally responsive teaching* (pp. 125–138). Mahwah, NJ: Erlbaum.

Smith, A. (1997). Cultural diversity and the coming-out process: Implications for clinical practice. In B. Greene (Ed.), *Ethnic and cultural diversity among lesbians and gay men* (pp. 279–300). Thousand Oaks, CA: Sage.

Sophie, J. (1985–1986). A critical examination of stage theories of lesbian identity development. *Journal of Homosexuality, 12*(2), 39–51. doi:10.1300/J082v12n02_03

Stinson, S. (2011). No simple answer to gay athlete issue. *The National Post.* Retrieved from http://www.nationalpost.com/opinion/columnists/simple+answer+athlete+issue/4820676/story.html

Stacey, J., & Biblarz, T. (2001). (How) does the sexual orientation of parents matter? *American Sociological Review, 66*, 159–183. Retrieved from: http://www.jstor.org/stable/2657413

Sun, C. (2010). *Letter to school officials regarding LGBT student privacy.* Retrieved from the American Civil Liberties Union website: http://www.aclu.org/lgbt-rights/letter-school-officials-regarding-lgbt-student-privacy

Szalacha, L. (2003). Safer sexual diversity climates: lessons learned from an evaluation of Massachusetts safe schools program for gay and lesbian students. *American Journal of Education, 110*, 58–88. Retrieved from http://www.jstor.org/action/showPublication?journalCode=amerjeduc

Szymanski, M. (2010). Bi book review: Bisexual books for youth audiences. *Journal of Bisexuality, 10*(4), 489–491. doi:10.1080/15299716.2010.521063

Taylor, W. (1994). *The blue lawn.* New York, NY: HarperCollins.

Tinker v. Des Moines Independent Community School District, 383 F.2d 988 (8th Cir. 1967)

Trolley, B., & Hanel, C. (2010). *Cyber kids, cyber bulling, cyber balance*. Thousand Oaks, CA: Corwin Press.

Valente, T. W., Ritt-Olson, A., Stacy, A., Unger, J. B., Okamoto, J., & Sussman, S. (2007). Peer acceleration: Effects of a social network tailored substance abuse prevention program among high risk adolescents. *Addiction, 102*(11), 1804–1815. doi:10.1111/j.1360-0443.2007.01992.x

Valenti, M. (2010). The roles of gay-straight alliance (GSA) advisors in public high schools. In C. Bertram, M. Crowley, & S. Massey (Eds.), *Beyond progress and marginalization: LGBTQ youth in educational contexts* (pp. 52–88). New York, NY: Peter Lang.

Valenti, M., & Campbell, R. (2009). Working with youth on LGBT issues: Why gay-straight alliance advisors become involved. *Journal of Community Psychology, 37*(2), 228–248. doi:10.1002/jcop

Vigna, J. (1995). *My two uncles*. Morton Grove, IL: Albert Whitman.

Vilain, E. (2006). Genetics of intersexuality. *Journal of Gay & Lesbian Psychotherapy, 10*(2), 9–26. doi:10.1300/J236v10n02_02

Wald, K., Rienzo, B., & Button, J. (2002). Sexual orientation of education politics: Gay and lesbian representation in American schools. *Journal of Homosexuality, 42*(4), 145–168. doi:10.1300/J082v42n04_10

Walker, A. (1982). *The color purple*. New York, NY: Pocket Books.

Walling, D. R. (2003). Gay and lesbian themed novels for classroom reading. *Journal of Gay and Lesbian Issues in Education, 1*(2), 97–108. doi:10.1300/J367v01n02_12

Watson, L., Varjas, K., Meyers, J., & Graybill, E. (2010). Gay-straight alliance advisors: Negotiating multiple ecological systems when advocating for LGBTQ youth. *Journal of LGBT Youth, 7*(2), 100–128. doi:10.1080/19361651003799700

Welcoming Schools. (n.d.). School climate assessment. Retrieved from the Welcoming Schools website: http://www.welcomingschools.org/wp-content/uploads/2010/07/Welcoming-Schools-School-Climate-Assessment.pdf

Whitman, J. S., & Boyd, C. J. (Eds.). (2003). *The therapist's notebook for lesbian, gay, and bisexual clients: Homework, handouts, and activities for use in psychotherapy*. Binghamton, NY: The Haworth Press.

Whitman, J. S., Horn, S. S., & Boyd, C. J. (2007). Activism in the schools: Providing LGBTQ affirmative training to school counselors. *Journal of Gay & Lesbian Psychotherapy, 11*(3), 143–154. doi:10.1300/J236v11n03_08

Whittaker, K. (2009). Gay-straight alliances and free speech: Are parental consent laws constitutional? *Berkeley Journal of Gender, Law, and Justice,* 48–67. Retrieved from http://genderlawjustice.berkeley.edu

Willard, N. (2007). *Cyberbullying and cyberthreats: Responding to the challenge of online social aggression, threats, and distress.* Champaign, IL: Research Press.

Williams, T. (1954). *Cat on a hot tin roof.* Sewanee, TN: The University of the South.

Williams, T. (1945). *The glass menagerie.* Sewanee, TN: The University of the South.

Wolfe, D. A., & Mash, E. J. (2006). Behavioral and emotional problems in adolescents: Overview and issues. In D. A. Wolfe & E. J. Mash (Eds.), *Behavioral and emotional disorders in adolescents: Nature, assessment, and treatment* (pp. 3–20). New York, NY: Guilford.

Yamanaka, L. A. (2000). *Name me nobody.* New York, NY: Hyperion Books for Children.

Young, E. L., & Mendez, L. M. R. (2003). The mental health professional's role in understanding, preventing, and responding to student sexual harassment. *Journal of Applied School Psychology, 19*(2), 7–23. doi:10.1300/J008v 19n02_02

Zamboni, B. D. (2006). Therapeutic considerations in working with the family, friends, and partners of transgendered individuals. *The Family Journal, 14*(2), 174–179. doi:10.1177/ 1066480705285251

Zucker, K. J. (2006). Gender identity disorder. In D. A. Wolfe & E. J. Mash (Eds.), *Behavioral and emotional disorders in adolescents: Nature, assessment, and treatment* (pp. 535–562). New York, NY: Guilford.

Zucker, K. J., & Cohen-Kettenis, P. T. (2008). Gender identity disorder in children and adolescents. In D. L. Rowland & L. Incrocci (Eds.), *Handbook of sexual and gender identity disorders* (pp. 376–422). Hoboken, NJ: Wiley.

Index

CD Contents